Chinese Fortune Sticks

Zhao Xiaomin
and Martin Palmer

Chinese Fortune Sticks

Consult the Ancient Oracle for Everyday Guidance

METRO BOOKS
NEW YORK

This 2008 edition published by Metro Books, by arrangement with Eddison Sadd Editions.

Metro Books
122 Fifth Avenue
New York, NY 10011

ISBN 978-1-4351-0978-0

1 3 5 7 9 10 8 6 4 2

Phototypeset in Carmina BT using QuarkXPress on Apple Macintosh
Bamboo sticks and shaker product of DH Resources, China
Printed and bound in China

Contents

INTRODUCTION 6

CHAPTER 1
CHINESE DIVINATION BY STICKS 8

CHAPTER 2
MESSENGERS OF WISDOM 16

CHAPTER 3
HOW TO USE THE FORTUNE STICKS 29
THE DIVINATION POEMS 34

CHAPTER 4
TAKING YOUR READING FURTHER –
THE I-CHING WAY 98

CHAPTER 5
HEARING THE VOICES –
UNDERSTANDING YOURSELF 105

FURTHER READING 112
ACKNOWLEDGMENTS 112

INTRODUCTION

Ironically, the greatest forms of Chinese divination rely entirely upon chance, on you having no influence over what happens. This is not the same as fate, which (as we shall see) has little place in Chinese divination. Instead, Chinese fortune-telling is based on chance, on abandonment of all attempts to control the future or your fate. It requires that you allow yourself to float free on the waters of chance and change, supported by the forces of yin and yang and travelling only the Way of the Tao – the Way of Nature.

Chinese culture is the longest, unbroken culture known to us. For at least 3,500 years, the core elements have either been in place or have been emerging. The Chinese language, the philosophy of what we now call Taoism, the wisdom of Confucian thought and order, the divination skills of fortune-telling, and the art of feng shui are all fruits of this vast and lengthy continuous culture of China. Rulers and dynasties have come and gone and will do so again, but the core elements of the Chinese understanding of life continue. It is from this rich stream that we shall be drawing in this book, as well as on traditions of divination that have remained unbroken but have been constantly developing for millennia.

A visit to a Chinese temple soon reveals what is important in Chinese life and belief. Numerous deities look down at you or, for the gods and goddesses of the underworld, literally look up at you! Shrines, altars and offering tables are to be found everywhere. Incense burners stand before the main altars, the smoke rising wistfully towards Heaven, bearing the prayers, hopes, and fears of those who have brought them and planted them into the soft sand of the incense burner. Offerings of fruit, cups of cold tea, and little bundles of cash are placed on offering trays before the most portentous deities, while the faithful line up to kneel and pray for help or guidance on the embroidered or patchwork cushion in front of the main deity.

But over and above all this, even over and above the sounds of the chanting, comes a distinctive sound – that of wooden sticks being shaken in a wooden or occasionally metal container. In front of statues, beside altars, in forecourts – in fact just about anywhere you can think of – people are seeking the guidance of the deities for their everyday life through the medium of pure chance, by putting themselves in touch with the flow of the Tao, the dynamic unity of yin and yang, and at the mercy of change. They abandon any attempt to reason or rationalize their way to an answer, not by seeking a definite answer so much as by seeking advice, a third eye or an alternative view on their problem – by using the divination sticks.

ABOUT THIS PACK

This pack provides you with your very own set of numbered fortune sticks and good luck stick-shaker so you too can enter the realms of Chinese tradition and tap into the Way of the Tao for help and advice on how to deal with the challenges of everyday modern life. In Chapter 1 we look at the sticks, and consider their meaning, their powers and their origins. Chapter 2 outlines the Chinese Way of the Tao and the complementary forces of yin and yang, also describing the life histories of the five deities whose wisdom speaks through the divination sticks. Chapter 3 describes how to use the sticks – the oldest of all the traditional divination methods of China – and outlines sixty-four divination poems inspired by the five main Chinese deities, together with their readings. Chapter 4 discusses how to make the most of your reading, combining it with the hexagrams of the I-Ching oracle. Chapter 5 concentrates on the reflective and meditational aspects of the divination system, and helps you to reflect on the visions and understanding of the world and yourself that emerge from the poems. You will soon discover how age-old Chinese wisdom can offer invaluable guidance for today.

CHAPTER 1

Chinese Divination by Sticks

What are the origins of the divination sticks? What exactly do they mean to the Chinese people? And how have the Chinese viewed the notions of fate, predestination and free will?

DIVINATION BY LOTS

Many of us have decided something by choosing lots. You collect a bunch of twigs or straws – enough for everyone taking part – and one straw or stick is shorter than all the others. Held hidden in the hand with just their tops poking out, all seemingly equal, they are presented to each person in turn. Everyone selects a straw or stick and whoever gets the shortest stick or straw is the 'loser'. Drawing lots in this way allows pure chance to guide us – it stops us trying to argue or work out a solution ourselves, instead allowing outside forces to select. Disagreement is eliminated, and change can occur through chance. This is a well-known concept in the West, existing in a variety of slightly different forms. For example, few people know how the successor to Judas Iscariot was chosen from among Jesus Christ's many followers: by throwing lots – using a form of divination sticks (see Acts of the Apostles 1.23–6). This seems to echo practices from the time of the Hebrew Bible (the Old Testament), where there are many instances of people casting lots to make decisions.

The Chinese divination sticks are a little like these lots – chosen at random and used to help resolve difficult issues. The randomness is seen as a form of guidance coming from a Higher Being, Power, or Place.

SEEKING GUIDANCE

In Jewish and Christian uses, it is believed that the external force that directs this random selection is God, but in Chinese divination the situation is more complicated. While the seeker will have prayed to a particular deity, such as those who have divination systems dedicated to them, in the end the seeker is not really looking to one deity for help but to be put in touch with the fundamental structure of the universe. This basic structure is the Tao – the Way of Nature, the way all things actually are in their real selves – and it is this that guides your decision-making, because the Tao guides and controls everything.

All Chinese divination is based on the insight of the oldest of all Chinese divination books, the I-Ching (*I-Ching* means 'The Book of Changes'). The book's title means life is essentially about change – not about clinging to what exists now, not about preserving tradition for its own sake. It is, instead, about the reality that, even in an apparently stable, traditional, and continuous culture, such as China's, change is inevitable. The Chinese skill of understanding that all life is change has somewhat ironically produced the longest-lasting culture in existence. That culture has seen many changes – empires falling and rising again – yet because of an acceptance of change the country has actually been able to survive all this. It is those cultures (and, therefore, those people) who cannot change who fear and resent change and who break under the pressure of its inevitability. This is well expressed in the classic text of Taoism – indeed, one of the greatest texts of Chinese wisdom – the Tao Te Ching. In Chapter 22 it says:

Learn to yield and be soft
If you want to survive.

Learn to bow
And you will stand in your full height.

Learn to empty yourself
and be filled by the Tao
... the way a valley empties itself into a river.

(translated by Kwok *et al.*)

Those who resist the forces of the Tao, of constant change, will be broken. Those who yield, bow, and allow themselves to be made by the experiences of change are the ones who will survive.

A seeker at a Chinese temple who uses the divination sticks to try to discover what their next action should be is not wanting safe answers. Instead, they are looking for guidance from the forces of change and chance, and want to know how to prepare for what is to come and how to be part of the changes that occur, rather than be someone who is overwhelmed by them. The Chinese understanding of fate is the key here.

FATE AND FREE WILL

Despite two thousand years of Christianity stressing free will, the West is still basically in thrall to the Greek notion of fate. Fate is something that is decreed from the day we are born, and nothing can change its course. Consider, for example, the classic story of Oedipus. Even before

he was born, the Fates said that Oedipus was fated to slay his own father and marry his mother, and from the day he was born, no matter what was done to try to avoid this, he fulfilled his fate.

This theme of the inevitability of fate runs like a destructive river through the Greek narratives and has fascinated and influenced Western thought deeply. Today, this fascination manifests itself in a mild form in those people who see their astrological signs as meaning they are a certain type of person, while others will go for a fortune reading and believe that because something has been foretold it has to come true.

It may be important to stress here that neither Western nor Chinese divination see its forecasts or insights as being about unchangeable fate – it was not for nothing that all the great medieval Christian courts had their own court astrologers. In true Western astrology, the horoscope tells you what is likely, not what is fated: you always have the ability within and around you to change your fate or fortune, and there is nothing inevitable in life. A fortune reading in Western astrology will tell you what is likely to happen to you, as a result of who you are now – if you stop being mean-minded or too generous, you can avoid the possible fate of being left friendless or of becoming bankrupt!

Fate does exist within Chinese divination, but it is very restricted. There are a few things that are given, and you have no control over them. You are fated to be born the sex you are and into a particular kind of family (wealthy, poor, sickly, exiled, and so on), and you are fated to be born on the day you are born. Beyond that, it is up to you. This type of fate is called *ming*.

Another word for fate – but one with very different connotations – is *yun*, which means 'to revolve, turn round, or go through a cycle'. It refers to the cycle of life from birth through youth, maturity, old age, and then death. In that sense, it talks about a largely fixed fate: you are born, grow older, then become old, and finally die. In some belief systems in China you may even be reborn, but not in all of them. But *yun* also means 'to change, to revolve, to turn upside down, to transform'. It carries with it the notion that within a fairly firm cycle, you have choices, chances, changes, and decisions you can make that will turn your life upside down. In the end, this may only mean that perhaps you die younger or older than you would have done otherwise.

So both *ming* and *yun* set out to define as fixed and immutable only the very basic framework of life. They are not talking about who you are or what you could be, because that is always, always, up to you.

One of the classic stories of fate and fortune illustrates this understanding beautifully *(see box opposite)*. The reading you may get today should be understood within the context of this story – at the end of the day it is *you* who makes the difference.

THE SAGE AND THE BOY

Long ago there lived a wise sage on a mountainside. This Taoist monk was skilled in the arts of divination, and people came to him from many miles away. One day the monk received a gift from someone he had helped. The gift was a young boy of about twelve, who was to be the monk's personal assistant. For some time the monk was too preoccupied to look properly at the boy, who did what he could but wasn't terribly useful.

One day the old monk looked deep into the face of the boy and, using his skills of face-reading, he was highly alarmed by what he saw: the boy was fated to die before he reached the age of thirteen. Moved by this revelation, the monk told the boy to travel home to see his family and not to return for three months. This would take the boy well beyond the date of his foretold demise.

Imagine the old monk's surprise when, three months later, the boy walked back up the mountain looking as fit and alive as could be. This time when the monk looked into the boy's face he saw that now he would live to a ripe old age. Sitting the boy down, the monk asked the boy to recount everything that had happened to him since he had left the mountain three months earlier.

The boy told of his journey down the mountainside. He explained how he had walked for a long while before he came to a stream, which was flooding and rising fast. He was about to wade his way across when he spotted a clump of dry land that was very soon to be covered by the rising flood level. On this tiny island-like clump he saw a large ants' nest, which was in turmoil as the ants tried in vain to save their eggs and their own lives. The young boy, moved by compassion, found a broken branch. He laid it across the swelling flood waters so it touched the tiny island at one end and lay on the dry grass on the other side. Holding it firm, he waited until all the ants had safely crossed over. Then he let go of the branch, which was swiftly swept up in the waters.

Thinking nothing of this, the boy continued on his way home.

The moment the old monk heard this, he knew what had happened to the boy. By his act of spontaneous compassion and generosity, the boy had revealed an aspect of his personality that had never been developed before. As a result, he had become a better person and would therefore live longer.

People often say 'But I'm a Monkey', or 'I can't help it, I'm a Rooster', referring to their Chinese animal sign, which is dependent on the year someone is born. But no Chinese man or woman believes that a person's animal sign determines who or what you are (your fate); it is just more likely you will have the characteristics of your birth sign, unless you decide to change.

CHOICE AND CHANGE VERSUS FATALISM

For a long while there has been a healthy disregard for the more silly and fateful predictions of those who like to claim that all is fixed at birth. As early as the third century BC, the philosopher Hsun Tzu was blasting away at the superstitious aspects of fate and fortune, in particular taking on those who said they could tell everything about a person from their appearance:

> *It would be much better to speak of the heart rather than examine their appearance, even better still to discuss people's intentions rather than the heart, for the heart is better than the countenance and a person's intention is better than even the heart. If someone's intention is good, so is their heart also.*
>
> *Even if people's looks are unfortunate, if their hearts are good then they are good people. Indeed, the reverse is true. A good-looking person can have a perverse and wicked heart …*
>
> *Thus, whether someone's outward appearance is good or bad, tall or short, gaunt or stocky, matters not a jot and has no influence upon fortune and good or bad. The ancients never talked of such nonsense and writers did not even mention it in their books.*

(*The Book of Hsun Tzu*, authors' translation)

The workings of the heart and conscience are more important than anything you are born with, though being born into a poor or traumatized family will be a handicap. That said, in the Chinese philosophy of fate, only fear and ignorance can hold you back.

Therefore, when you come to obtain your reading do not view it as definitive – see it as challenging you to change the situation by not doing what it predicts you will do.

WHERE DO DIVINATION STICKS COME FROM?

The origins of this distinctive Chinese system of divination sticks are lost in time, but we can speculate about some of their roots.

Each divination stick is flat, originally often made from strips of finely cut bamboo. Nowadays they are more likely to be made from very light, thin wood. The number of that particular stick is written in Chinese characters at the top. Some sets of divination sticks can have as many as a hundred sticks. Many have only fifty or so. We have chosen to use a set of sixty-four sticks, for reasons explored later *(see page 14)*. We can find a clue to their origins by looking at their shape and the way the characters are written down the strips.

The earliest Chinese books, from perhaps before 1000 BC, were written on thin strips of bamboo or wood, just like the divination sticks in this pack. They were strung together at the top and bottom and folded out like a bamboo latticed screen. Before paper was invented, around the time of Christ, all Chinese writings were produced on books made of these thin strips. Often they were only just wide enough for one character to be written across, while of course many characters could be written running downward, and this is why traditional Chinese books are read from top to bottom and not left to right. Interestingly, the invention of paper did not break this tradition of writing in strips.

These strip books were very troublesome: not only were they clumsy to use, but there was also the problem of what happened if the string holding the strips together broke. At one point, almost all the books in existence were destroyed by order of the terrible but mighty First Emperor of China (221–209 BC). Scholars tried to save the threatened books by burying them in the ground or hiding them in the hollowed-out sections of walls. Lost for many years, they were often rediscovered by accident, sometimes hundreds of years later, and by then most of the strings holding the texts together had been eaten by insects or rotted. The books may have been found, but often no one knew the order the strips were to be assembled in. The Tao Te Ching illustrates this problem perfectly: each chapter is quite short, and there is a great deal of repetition or many similar-sounding verses, so scholars have had to guess their proper order – something that is still debated today.

To imagine what a bamboo or wooden strip from one of these books looked like, simply pick up one of the divination sticks in your pack. In other words, one of the origins of the divination strip is the written strip. It is even possible that in the past the poem was written on such strips as well. These days the poems are printed, and only the number is printed on the stick (as it is on the sticks in this pack), but the link between stick and words is clear.

The Yarrow Sticks of the I-Ching

The I-Ching was consulted using yarrow sticks, another root of the divination stick. Yarrow is a wild plant, common around the world in various forms. It also seems to have a worldwide association with divination and with spells, magic, and the supernatural. In Anglo-Saxon

Britain it was considered to be a powerful divination and healing plant, and in China has been viewed for at least three thousand years as a particularly powerful divination aid. Indeed, the Shu Ching (Book of History written around 700 BC) says they were in use in the Hsia dynasty (around 2000–1700 BC). This may be why the plant is so commonly available and so easily turned into sticks (its leaves can be pushed off with no trouble and are good to cook with).

Confucius is supposed to have written The Great Treatise (one of the Commentaries accompanying the I-Ching), which gives a number of detailed instructions for using yarrow sticks to obtain a reading, including manipulating them to get a figure of six lines (hexagram). The number of the hexagram (there are sixty-four in total) is looked up in the book, and it is this that gives you your reading.

Even by the time of Confucius, yarrow sticks seem to have given way to easier methods of manipulation, but their use was still kept for special occasions. So closely was Confucius associated with the yarrow stick method that it was claimed that the most auspicious sticks to use were those made from plants growing on his tomb in Qufu. This claim seems rather ironic when you consider that Confucius said that he had no views on the supernatural, gods, or the afterlife because he had enough to do dealing with the present reality of living!

The association of the yarrow sticks with the I-Ching certainly set the model for the role of similar, though not identical, use of divination sticks with other fortune-telling books. It is easy to see how the divination sticks, combined with the writing strips, came into being.

Oracle Bones

The last source of inspiration for the creation of divination sticks comes from a very different origin: the earliest-known forms of Chinese divination are the use of ox shoulder bones and tortoise or turtle shells.

The process is a peculiar one and was used throughout the era of the Shang dynasty (around 1700–1100 BC) and by the early Zhou dynasty (around 1100–900 BC). The shell or bone was scored with notches on its underside, then a heated rod was applied to the notched mark. The heat caused the thinned shell or bone to crack on the other side, producing lines, and these were then 'read' as an answer to the divination question being asked. If the answer turned out to be true or valid, the bones were marked up more clearly and kept as records. More than 150,000 bones have been found in the last hundred years, and the search for meaning in the lines on the oracle bones helps us to see why Chinese is essentially a pictorial written language. The cracks were seen to depict what they spoke about, so three wavy lines were read to mean a river. The very origins of Chinese writing and characters lie in divination.

The notches on the shells or bone were usually made in a series of lines running from top to bottom, so the notched lines also bear a close resemblance to strips. So, in yet another way, the elongated strip has its roots at the very beginnings of recorded Chinese divination.

It is impossible to say exactly when the use of divination sticks came into prominence as a form of divination. Certainly they have been the staple of temple divination for more than five hundred years. One of the most famous of the divination poem series, those of Kuan Yin *(see page 22)*, date from the fourteenth century and from their earliest recorded appearance were always used with sticks. It is likely that this highly simple and effective method was much loved by ordinary peasants down the centuries of Chinese history. Other methods – coins, special tokens, and so on – were for more elite or city-based systems. For example, the Ling Ch'i Ching uses a system of twelve tokens, representing (in sets of four) Heaven, Humanity, and Earth, also called Upper, Middle, and Lower.

While the Ling Ch'i Ching has been popular since its composition in the third-to-fourth centuries AD as a sort of poor man's I-Ching, today it is not found as extensively as divination stick systems. The sticks' simplicity is their main appeal, together with the fact that this simplicity makes it clear that you cannot influence your reading. In many Western versions of the I-Ching, for example, a sort of interference is allowed through the system of changing lines, but this is not how the Chinese have traditionally used the system. Indeed, for many Chinese consulting the I-Ching, Ling Ch'i Ching, or the books of divination poems, it is enough simply to close your eyes, open any of the books just mentioned at random, and read whatever your eye falls upon first.

The Divination Sticks go West

As the Chinese have spread out into the wider world over the last 150 years in what is called the Chinese diaspora, they have taken the divination stick system with them. Indeed, the sticks are used by non-Chinese around the world because they can be used and understood so easily. We have found antique divination sticks in Sri Lanka, San Francisco and Amsterdam, for example. But a Chinese person is always to be by their side to translate and interpret the divination poems. With the translated poems in this pack, you can enjoy the ancient system of Chinese divination sticks with no need for extra help.

CHAPTER 2

Messengers of Wisdom

But who exactly is speaking through the fortune sticks? And who are the deities that have provided the wisdom you can now access through this book?

YIN, YANG, AND TAO

The Chinese believe that there is no one supreme deity or being ruling the cosmos. Instead, they believe that there is one natural way of being, the Way of the Tao. From the Tao, come the two main natural forces of the universe: yin and yang. These two forces are complete opposites: yin is cold, wet, winter, earthy, female, dark, and watery; yang is hot, dry, summer, heavenly, male, light, and fiery. Between them they contain and are contained in everything that exists. Both seek total control, and because of this, they are locked in a perpetual battle, which is where the dynamic power of existence comes from. While yin can sometimes seem to be in the ascendancy – when floods come, or when the cold, wet, dark nights of winter are upon us, for example – it cannot be completely triumphant. The reason for this is best seen in the yin/yang symbol itself. At the heart of each there is a drop of the other: inside the yin is a spot of yang; inside the yang, a spot of yin. The seeds of their eventual waning are revealed at the precise moment of their waxing.

This is well-illustrated by the seasons. Winter is yin, and at the height of winter it is hard, perhaps even impossible, to imagine that summer will come and things will change as a result. Yet at the point of winter's depths the turn is already happening, leading eventually to spring and summer. Equally, when summer (with all its yang force) is upon us, it is difficult to imagine the coolness of winter, but when summer is at its zenith the seeds of change are already sown, and autumn and winter inexorably follow. In traditional Chinese culture, the Emperor, the symbol of humanity's pivotal role in helping to keep the balance between yin and yang, would pray to the yin force in the heights of summer and to the yang forces in the depths of winter.

From the battling yet strangely complementary forces of yin and yang comes ch'i – the life breath, or energy. All that lives, lives because ch'i flows through it. Ch'i is the invigorating energy, the breath of life bringing the inanimate to life. Taoists believe that when you are born you contain within you all the ch'i you will have for the rest of your life. Every time you breathe out, you lose a little ch'i. Thus some Taoists are very careful with what they eat so they do not create wind, because that lets a lot of your vital life ch'i out!

THE TAO – ORIGIN OF ALL

The Chinese cosmological worldview, then, is not one of a supreme deity but of supreme forces that are linked, natural and all-powerful, and we go against them at our peril. The Chinese cosmological worldview is beautifully captured in Chapter 42 of the Tao Te Ching in what is in essence the Creed of Traditional Chinese Thought:

The Tao
gives birth to the Origin;
The Origin
gives birth to the Two;
The Two
give birth to the Three –
The Three give birth to every living thing.

All things are held in yin and carry yang:
And they are held together in the ch'i of teeming energy.

(adapted from Kwok *et al.*)

Here the Tao is seen as being before the origin of all, while the term 'the Two' refers, of course, to yin and yang. The 'Three' alludes to Heaven, Earth, and Humanity.

ASKING YOUR QUESTION

When you seek advice from the divination sticks, therefore, you are asking advice of the cosmos and all that is natural and vast, complex and interactive within it, and this is why the answer you receive will ask things of you. If you want to know which horse is going to win this afternoon's race or what the weather will be like on Monday, this is not the right book for you. But the book *will* help you if you are trying to work out what to do with your life, with your relationships and commitments – not that it will give you answers as such, since the cosmos is not in the habit of doing that! What it will do is briefly, tantalizingly, reintegrate you with the natural flow of the cosmos so you can look anew at your supposedly massive and insurmountable hurdle and see, in the order of all things, in the light of the cosmos, that it might not be quite the enormous problem you thought it was.

THE GODS AND GODDESSES OF CHINA

The Chinese always like a human face or a personality to deal with, but when Buddhism came to China in the first-to-third centuries AD, it came in its pure Theravadian way. This early form of Buddhism stressed that there were no deities from whom help could be expected – not even the Buddha. What the Buddha taught, it said, was a path that everyone could set out on to discover their own way to find release from the horrors of reincarnation.

Within a few centuries the Chinese had worked on Buddhism and made it more acceptable and workable for their culture. The core philosophy was still there for those who were interested, but around it had grown thousands of deities, tens of thousands of spiritual beings, Buddhas not just of this age but of countless ages before and after, salvation Buddhas, and bodhisattvas – those able to reach Nirvana but who delay doing so through compassion for suffering beings (*see page 23*) who could save you from reincarnation through good deeds and prayer. It was now a Buddhism with many thousands of faces.

While founding itself upon the yin/yang philosophy, traditional Chinese religion has also created one of the most extraordinary hierarchies of deities known to religion – and for a very practical reason. The deities give a human face to the profound concepts of Chinese philosophy: for many ordinary worshippers the deities are the Tao, but beyond this there is always the challenge of seeing through the personalities of the deities and encountering the force of the Tao they embody.

The Taoist pantheon used to resemble the Imperial Order of Emperors, Empresses, officials in charge of cities and regions, and ministers charged with responsibility for welfare, housing, the army, and so on. It has at its nominal head the Jade Emperor and his Consort, below whom are ranked such deities as the Town God, the City God, the District God, the God who protects from smallpox, the God of the Drains, the Thunder God, and the Gods and Goddesses of Childbirth. There is a God of War and a God of Scholars, and in the Underworld there are Ten Judges of the Dead, who punish the dead for the misdemeanours of their life according to strict rules.

This Heavenly reproduction of the Imperial systems is hardly surprising, for throughout the centuries many of the gods and goddesses were appointed to their roles by the Emperors. They were frequently real people who had lived good or worthy lives and who, when they died, were assigned to look after some division of Heaven that tallied with the roles they had played in this life. We will encounter some of these gods and goddesses later in this chapter (*see pages 20–28*), since many of the divination poems that are featured in this book come from their traditions.

Buddhism did not have quite the same relationship with the Imperial Order. However, it too developed a multitude of Buddhas, bodhisattvas, protector deities, and the like in order to make Buddhist ideas more easily understandable to the ordinary person. Buddhist Hells, for example, outdid the Taoist Hells by having eighteen different ones, each with its own Judge and officials.

Beyond the Deities – the Ultimate

Beyond and behind these pantheons there was always something deeper. In both Buddhism and Taoism this was expressed physically in statues of the three key deities. The three main deities in Buddhism (almost always found at the heart of a temple) are the Buddha of the Past, the Present, and the Future. They symbolize the sense of time conveyed by Buddhism, the ageless aeons during which great teachers (Buddhas) come time after time. The Buddha of the Past sits with hands resting together – his work is done. The Buddha of the Present holds his hands in the mode of teaching – he still tries to break through our ignorance and wants to reach us with the truth of the teachings, which can lead us away from suffering and rebirth. The Buddha of the Future sits ready to start teaching.

The three Taoist deities are called the Three Pure (or Bright, or Luminous) Ones. First of all they represent the Tao as pure beingness, the origin of origins. The second statue represents the Tao as word incarnate, and is usually Lao Tzu, the supposed author of the Tao Te Ching (the Taoist classic) and spiritual founder of the main branch of Taoist religion today. The final image is of the Tao as the Yellow Emperor, the personification of Tao as ruler of this world. There are other variations upon these three. For example, there is one clearly based upon Buddhism: the Original Tao; there is the Tao as the Jade Emperor, protector of the present; and also the Tao of the Jade Dawn of the Golden Era – the future Tao.

In both Buddhism and Taoism, these collections of three point beyond themselves, beyond the carved faces, the golden statues, to the truths that each faith tries to present about the origin, meaning, purpose and direction of all life. And it is towards this that the divination sticks are also directing you. Do not get hung up on the individual deities, but on the messages they bring.

Creating This Pack

When we discussed the idea of this pack with Chinese divination friends, and particularly the combining of readings from different sources, they were skeptical. They questioned whether it was right to put together different readings from different deities, even if, as we have

done, we kept the readings in the numerical position they hold in their original texts. We responded that surely the whole point of divination was to be put in touch with the Ultimate Force of the Universe – be that the Tao, Buddha nature or, in the Jewish and Christian traditions, God. Unless we encountered this power in every divination system, there was little point in using them, we said. Our friends had to concede that we were right.

THE FIVE DEITIES

It is now time to introduce you to the deities through whose poems and insights you can be in touch with deeper and more profound forces. We have selected poems from five different sources. Each poem stands in the numerical place it occupies in its original book – so, for example, poem number 5, taken from the poems of Immortal Wong Tai, is also poem 5 in the full text of his divination poems.

The five deities through whom the Divine, the Ultimate, or the Tao speaks are:

- Kuan Ti – the God of War and Literature
- Kuan Yin – the God/Goddess of Compassion and Mercy
- Wong Tai – the Immortal, God of the Poor
- Cheng Huang – the City God and Protector
- The Jade Emperor – Ruler of Heaven.

What follows is a brief life history of each of the five deities, together with an explanation of how they earned their place in the Chinese divination system.

Kuan Ti – God of War and Literature

Kuan Ti is one of the most extraordinary of deities, illustrating the idea that a human being who does great deeds can be elevated over time until he or she becomes an Emperor in Heaven.

Kuan Ti was born as Kuan Yu in AD 162. He started life very humbly as a seller of bean curd. But while he was undertaking this lowly job, he also studied every night and gradually became an accomplished scholar. A massively strong man, he soon ran into trouble with officialdom in the decaying and corrupt last stages of the great Han dynasty: he murdered a cruel magistrate who was forcing a young woman into his harem against her will, despite the best efforts of her aged parents to prevent the magistrate. The injustice of the situation moved Kuan Yu to action, setting a pattern that would shape the rest of his life.

One day he picked a fight with a strongman butcher who had laid down a challenge to see if anyone passing could lift a great stone. When Kuan Yu lifted it, the butcher attacked him, and the two were only separated by a third strongman, an itinerant seller of straw sandals. These three strongmen then became the closest of friends, and in a peach orchard, they took an oath always to defend each other. This took place in AD 191 and marked the beginning of the rise of the three friends – one of them, the straw-sandal seller Lie Pei, was eventually to become ruler of the State of Shu, while the other two became leading generals in his army.

Kuan Yu kept the oath, even though he was offered political and military power by one of the other contenders for the throne. This led to the events that brought him as a prisoner before the man who had offered him such power, and when he still refused to betray his two comrades, Kuan Yu and his son were put to death in AD 220.

The core elements of his divinization are already clear: a strongman who was also a scholar; a loyal friend who would die rather than betray an oath; a compassionate man who used his strength to defend the weak and powerless. All these were to be magnified in later centuries as virtuous, and he brought these elements together to answer the prayers of the faithful.

In 1120 the Emperor decreed that Kuan Yu was to be appointed as Faithful and Loyal Duke in the hierarchy of Heaven, where it had long been assumed he put his military skills at the service of the Jade Emperor *(see page 27)*. In 1128 he was further elevated in Heaven by an Imperial decree that said he was now to be known as the Magnificent Prince and Pacifier. He was further raised in the hierarchy in 1132 by having the title 'Warrior Prince and Civilizer' added.

In 1594 he was made Faithful and Loyal Great Emperor in Heaven – Kuan Ti – God of War and of Literature. In 1813 he is supposed to have saved the Emperor from an assassination attempt, and forty years later, he was seen leading the Imperial troops into battle against the revolutionary Taiping movement. In recent years he has also become a god of wealth and success and is the second-most popular deity to be found in Chinese shops, workshops, restaurants, and homes.

DEITY OF THE PEOPLE

For fairly obvious reasons, Kuan Ti has become the patron deity of martial arts societies and clubs, and his image can be seen all over China and

throughout the Chinese diaspora. His is the classic case of a real man-made god and a typical example of how the deities in Heaven have arisen. Despite being closely linked to the Imperial Cult – for example, the sword of the public executioner in each city was kept in his temple – he has passed through the fires of Republicanism and Communism to reappear even more devoutly followed. His divination poems are very common in China and can be found on sale outside all the main Taoist and Buddhist temples. He is essentially a Taoist-cum-Confucian deity with no links to Buddhism, though this does not stop Buddhist temples from having shrines to him.

Statues and pictures of him usually show Kuan Ti seated, wearing robes and armor, with a huge black beard, and looking sternly straight ahead, one hand pulling his long beard to one side. Behind him stand his faithful attendants. To the right (looking at the picture or statue) is his son Kuan Ping, who was executed with him and is thus the model of the faithful to death, and Chou Chang, his attendant who died fighting at his side and always carries his halberd. Sometimes there will also be Kuan Ti's faithful war horse Red Hare, who refused to leave the body of his master and died of starvation while standing guard over the corpse. A beautiful poem sums up the Chinese love and respect for this great man and deity:

Without equal was our Lord Kuan,
Above all others he rose up, the best amongst the best,
Godlike and terrible in war, he was kindly and gentle in peace.
Glorious as the sun at noon,
Radiant as the noblest of all times,
He remains, the illumination of all others, for all ages,
A sign of virtue to every generation.

(*Romance of the Three Kingdoms*, translated by C.H. Brewitt-Taylor)

Plays, operas, and dramas based on the story of Kuan Ti and his two sworn brothers have been – and still are – immensely popular, as is the account of their adventures, the best-selling novel *Romance of the Three Kingdoms* – a marvelous narrative, which is available in some good English translations. Further details on Kuan Ti can be found in *Essential Chinese Mythology* *(see page 112 for further details)*.

Kuan Yin – God/Goddess of Compassion and Mercy

Kuan Shih Yin – usually shortened to just Kuan Yin – is the most popular deity in China today. Her story is even more extraordinary than that of Kuan Ti, and her poems of divination are just as popular.

Kuan Shih Yin means 'the one who hears the cries of the world.' She is the compassionate, merciful, loving saviour deity supreme of China, who plucks her followers from danger in this life and the next. Originally Buddhist, long ago she transcended the bounds of any one faith, for her origins lie as much in Taoism and Christianity as they do in Buddhism.

When Buddhism arrived in China in the early centuries after Christ, it came with the whole baggage of austere teachings and entirely male-dominated hierarchies of divine beings. It was the Mahayana version of Buddhism in the sixth-to-seventh centuries that really caught the attention and devotion of ordinary people. This was the salvationary Buddhism of bodhisattvas (beings who, through countless lives of blameless living, generous actions, and good karma, have now reached a point at which they could cease to be, cease rebirth, and thus could enter Nirvana) and of Amida Buddha.

Unlike classical Buddhism with its emphasis on self-realization and following the ascetic path of the historical Buddha, the salvationary Buddhism offered a way to escape the terrors of rebirth and karma. Devout prayers to the correct bodhisattvas or Buddhas could ensure that you would be reborn in Paradise. However, these compassionate ones hold back from this final step in order to help as many of the suffering creatures of the world to escape as possible. They literally pluck the faithful from Hell and bring them safely into Paradise.

One of the most popular of the bodhisattvas who came with the religion from India is known as Avalokitesvara. This male deity is recorded as having the power to become whatever is necessary to reach a troubled soul. In the beautiful *Lotus Sutra*, which is where Avalokitesvara is first recorded, he is able to become a Hindu, a nun or a monk, or himself. Avalokitesvara is loved, in particular, because he can save the faithful from very real troubles – for example, being mugged, kidnapped, or burgled – as well as from the horrors of Hell and rebirth.

When the *Lotus Sutra* arrived in China, 'Avalokitesvara' was translated as 'Kuan Shih Yin' and the devotion to Kuan Yin began, the rise of which is truly quite remarkable. In a period of one hundred years, inscriptions in the Buddha caves of central China shifted from a situation where the vast

A THOUSAND ARMS, A THOUSAND EYES

She was the youngest daughter of a powerful king. From her earliest days, she showed herself to be different, caring for all creatures and only ever wanting to be a Buddhist nun. Her father wished to marry her to a neighboring king, but she refused and insisted on becoming a nun. At last her father gave in, but he told the abbess of the nunnery to give her as hard a time as possible and to include all the most disgusting jobs. Despite this (indeed, perhaps because of this), she was blissfully happy.

Her father was furious and, in his anger, sent his army to burn the nunnery to the ground. They sacked the nunnery, murdered many nuns, then set fire to the ruins. Kuan Yin put out the fire with Heaven's help, but was seized by the army general and brought before her father. His anger had grown to madness, and he ordered that she be executed, but the sword bent around her neck and eventually the executioner had to strangle her with a silk cord. As soon as the breath left her body, a huge tiger leaped into the court, seized Kuan Yin and took her off to a forest. Her soul descended to Hell, but wherever she appeared Hell turned into Paradise. The King of all the Hells, Yama, decided she must be returned to life or Hell itself would be destroyed. When her body and soul were reunited, she took refuge on an isolated mountain and there practiced meditation for many years.

Meanwhile the girl's father fell dangerously ill. He was told that he could only be healed if someone voluntarily gave their arms and eyes to cure him, and that only one such being existed, on a mountain far away. Not realizing it was his daughter, he sent a messenger, never believing such an act of selfless giving could happen. Kuan Yin gave her arms and her eyes to help her father, and he was healed. In order to thank the one who had saved him, he travelled to the mountain, and the moment he saw his disfigured daughter he realized the full extent of his awful behavior. He knelt down to worship her, and at that moment, she revealed herself to be the goddess Kuan Yin. Her father repented and became a model king.

Kuan Yin is sometimes depicted with a thousand arms and eyes and is often known as the Thousand Armed, Thousand Eyed Kuan Yin, which refers to what her father did to celebrate his daughter. The story says how he told an official to command a sculptor to create a statue of Kuan Yin, saying that the statue should have 'no arms, no eyes'. But the words for this particular form of 'no' and the word for 'thousand' sound almost identical, and the poor sculptor worked for nine months carving a statue with a thousand arms and eyes. Imagine everyone's astonishment when the statue was unveiled before the king!

It is a delightful story, nicely capturing Kuan Yin's fun and informality. Today she can be found in most Chinese homes and temples (Buddhist or Taoist). Having ruled Macau for 450 years, the Portuguese funded a sixty-five-foot statue of her in Macau as a parting gift – such is her ability to reach across cultures and faiths as a symbol of divine love and compassion.

majority of them depicted the historical Buddha to one where most depicted Kuan Shih Yin instead.

An even more remarkable change happened sometime in the eighth-to-ninth centuries – Kuan Yin changed sex. Prior to the eighth century, there are no female images, but by the tenth century almost every image is female, and Kuan Yin was well on her way to the supreme position of devotion and love she holds to this day. Through a combination of influences from Taoism and Christianity, both of which were highly active in China at this time, the austere male Buddhism of India was transformed by the Chinese.

Over the centuries Kuan Yin has also absorbed many local Taoist and shamanic female deities. She is clearly a vastly complex figure, but it is her role as protector, bringer of children, and the very embodiment of mercy for which she is most well-known.

There are hundreds of legends told about her (*see Further Reading on page 112 for collections of her stories*), but the one opposite is perhaps the most famous and best captures her role as the goddess of compassion.

Wong Tai – the Immortal, God of the Poor

The Immortal Wong Tai (in Chinese, *Wong Tai Sin*) is a very different kind of deity. Almost unknown until the twentieth century, he is a Cantonese deity whose major temple and shrine is found in Hong Kong, yet because of the immense influence of Hong Kong Chinese on the wider Chinese world, he has spread far and wide. He is not as well-known as Kuan Ti and Kuan Yin, but his divination poems are highly influential and are typical of poems associated with local deities.

His own account of his origins and fate are recorded in writings revealed to his followers, along with the poems ascribed to him. His family was very poor, and between the ages of eight and fifteen he had to work as a shepherd in the south of China, near Canton. At the age of fifteen, he met an immortal, who gave him an elixir of immortality, and for forty years he was lost to his family while he lived the life of an immortal sage. Eventually his brother found him and asked him what had happened to the sheep he was meant to be looking after. Wong Tai took his brother back to

the hillside where he had left them forty years ago. Large boulders covered the hillside, and when Wong Tai called out, they returned to being sheep. His brother, duly impressed, also trained and became an immortal. The fate of the sheep, however, is undisclosed.

This story is set at the time of the Jin dynasty, around AD 266 to 316. There is an account written in the fourth century AD of an immortal known as Wong Cho Ping, and it is clear that the Wong Tai story derives from that. However, only in the last hundred years has this otherwise quite obscure Taoist immortal taken off to become one of the major regional deities of China.

Wong Tai is particularly linked with medicine, and the association that supports the main temple in Hong Kong, the Sik Sik Yuen, gives free medicine, runs clinics, and provides schools for the poor. He has become almost a god of the poor because his is a classic rags-to-riches story. Today, people in Hong Kong and Hong Kong Chinese worldwide consult Wong Tai on everything from marriage to health to careers. Of all the temples in Hong Kong, the Wong Tai Sin temple has the greatest number of professional fortune-tellers, who rent stalls in the temple compound, the revenue from which goes towards the funds available for charitable work provided by the Sik Sik Yuen. (*See Further Reading on page 112 for more information on Wong Tai.*)

Cheng Huang – the City God and Protector

The fourth deity is Cheng Huang, known as the City God and the Celestial Mandarin. His name is a wonderful example of a deity formed from a firm reality but used to express a profound spiritual vision. The city walls of China are still a major feature of the land and, although many have been demolished in the last sixty years or so, many still remain. For example, the great city wall of Xian in central China runs for ten-and-a-half miles around the city, and it is so broad that two double-decker buses could easily drive down it and still leave space for thousands of pedestrians on either side. These walls are known as *cheng*. They are constructed by building two walls running parallel to each other and then filling in the space between, which can be from anywhere up to about thirty feet, with rammed earth. The earth is dug from just outside the city wall and thus creates a deep moat or ditch running round the wall. This is known as a *huang*. Thus the City God's name is a combination of 'wall' and 'moat', a double defense, and this is how Cheng Huang is viewed – as providing a defense against both natural disasters and human greed and corruption.

The City God is one of the oldest deities of China, predating Confucianism, Taoism, and Buddhism. Legends say that the great Emperor Yao (who is supposed to have ruled around 2300 BC) ordered the first sacrifices to the City God. In classical Chinese thought, the City God complements the just magistrate, who has temporal power over the city. The City God has spiritual power and is the yin to the magistrate's yang.

While the City God is believed to be an essential spiritual force, it has long been the custom of the people of a city to elect a recently deceased, good and just man to be their particular embodiment of the City God, who is worshipped for protection, security, peace, an end to plagues and for the general well-being of the people. Much suppressed under Communism in China, Cheng Huang is slowly making his way back into favor in China.

Cheng Huang is sometimes depicted sitting down like a judge, with four attendants who carry out his orders to arrest wrongdoers or to bring to justice those who have committed crimes against the people. Two of these attendants are animal-faced, known as Ox Head and Horse Face. The others are contrasting figures, representing the forces of yin and yang, and are known as Master White and Master Black. These four attendants ensure that if anyone escapes justice in this life they suffer in one of the Ten Taoist (or Eighteen Buddhist) Hells after death.

This is a god who expects good behavior and rewards justice. He also protects the weak and vulnerable and is a more fiery, righteous, and judgmental counterpart to the unconditional compassion of Kuan Yin.

One of the most famous of all City Gods is Yue Fei, from the beautiful ancient city of Hangzhou, once the capital of China. A famous twelfth-century-AD general, he tried to warn the Emperor of the treachery of his senior ministers who were hand in hand with invading Mongolians. The Emperor chose to believe the traitors rather than Yue Fei and had him executed. The truth came out later, and Yue Fei was posthumously rewarded by being made the City God of Hangzhou.

The Jade Emperor – Ruler of Heaven

Last, but by no means least, is the Jade Emperor. Jade is a most auspicious gem in China, standing for absolute purity and immortality. It is the most favored of all the gems and is often exchanged at marriages in order to symbolize the permanence of the wedding vows. The

Emperor is, of course, the highest possible position in the Empire; thus the combination of the two facets indicates someone of the highest purpose and authority.

Yet the Jade Emperor is a relatively recent Chinese deity. He was first created by the (then) human Emperor in AD 1012 as a support to a failing dynasty and as a Taoist alternative to the Buddha. The Emperors of the next few centuries heaped honorific titles upon the Jade Emperor, making him the supreme authority in Heaven and furnishing him with power over all the other deities. Indeed, so great was his popularity among the ordinary people that soon Taoism depicted the Jade Emperor as the literal Emperor of all deities – including Buddhist ones – and as being seated enthroned with the gods ranked all around. There is a wonderful description of the Jade Emperor (if slightly unflattering at times, since it was written by a Buddhist) in the novel *Monkey* (*see Further Reading on page 112 for more details*).

His popularity has waned somewhat in recent years, because the earthly version of his Imperial Court has been destroyed and discredited, first by the Republicans and then the Communists. But his genial image and his role as a sort of benevolent grandfather figure has meant that the Jade Emperor has begun to reappear again, and his poems of divination are increasingly being sought and used.

These are the five sources we have drawn upon to offer you a unique set of divination poems and inspirations. Now we need to discover how to use the divination sticks and reveal the secrets contained within the sixty-four poems associated with them.

CHAPTER 3

How to Use the Fortune Sticks

Using the fortune sticks could not be easier, but you should not approach this lightly. Before consulting them, you must consider which questions to ask them and what exactly you want the sticks to tell you. It is also advisable to prepare yourself both physically and mentally before you embark on a reading.

ASKING THE RIGHT QUESTIONS

To begin with, ask yourself if you really need the help of the deities and the Tao behind them. Are you bringing the wrong sort of query or request to the sticks? They will not answer your questions with a direct answer, apart from in the most exceptional of cases, nor will they respond to the wrong kind of questions.

For example, do you want an instant decision on something of relatively minor significance? This could be whether to take your raincoat with you today or not; whether to buy one kind of product or another; whether to play the lottery or gamble on a particular horse; whether to stay at home or go out to a party. These are questions which you need simply to have common sense about; you should know yourself well enough to answer them without outside help. The divination sticks will not help you here.

Maybe you have a serious question but are simply asking the wrong authority. For example, you could be seriously ill, and up till now have tried to ignore the fact. Do not ask the divination sticks what to do. It is vital you visit a doctor and get expert help instead. If you are feeling down, again the sticks will not be able to help you. Perhaps you could ring a helpline, speak to a counselor or just call your best friend and talk to *them* about what is happening in your life. Even if you feel that the sticks can help, you should always seek other views, other forms of assistance and guidance. Do not rely merely on the sticks for guidance because that is not what they are for.

Having said all this, they can be of immense help and are particularly useful when you have considered all sides of an issue and simply cannot decide which way to go. The sticks allow you to stop trying to reason your way to a solution and instead offer a chance to stand back and look at things afresh. Then, perhaps seeking other suitable advice,

you can move forward in making a decision. Remember that the Tao is natural – it carries with it that which is natural and right, and rejects that which is selfish and wrong. The deities invoked are all symbols of mercy, compassion, care, authority, and judgment. You will receive some measure of all in the poems you are given. Listen carefully to the varied layers and images offered to you.

MINDFUL PREPARATION

Having settled on the question you want to put to the Tao, you then need to get yourself ready. There is nothing magical in this, and if you simply do not have time, you can go straight to using the sticks. But if you do have time, it is a good idea to prepare yourself. You should calm yourself and wash your hands and face – not for any magical reason, but because you are going visiting. You are calling upon the Tao and coming face to face with the deities, so you need to get yourself ready for this.

Find a comfortable place to sit and spend a few minutes thinking about your question. Do you already know the answer, in fact? Or, more worryingly, do you know what you *want* the answer to be? If your answer is yes, take time to clear your mind so you can be receptive. Think about the issues and people involved in the question you wish to raise. Allow their hopes and fears, their needs and gifts, to be in your mind and see if this alters the way you want to phrase the question. You are not just an individual; the Tao sees you as part of the flow of all life. Remember this as you prepare to ask for advice.

USING THE STICKS

When you are ready, either say the question out loud or write it down. You are now ready to take up the divination sticks. Hold the shaker firmly in both hands, and tilt it away from you until it is at an angle of about ninety degrees *(see below left)*. Begin to shake the container up and down slowly so the sticks start to shift up the tube and out of the container. As they get closer and closer to falling out, tilt the shaker

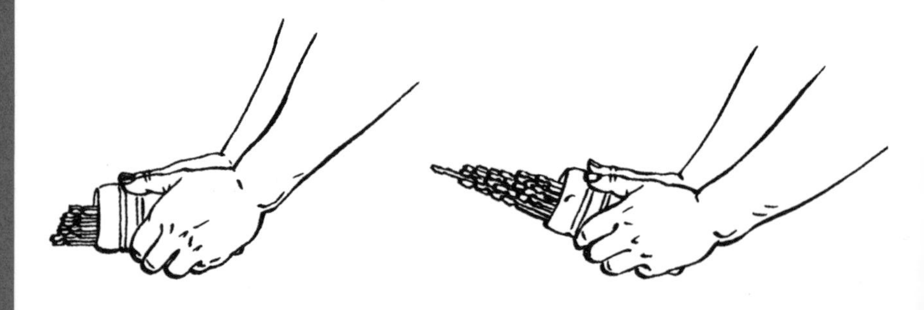

back a little so only a few sticks are poking out *(see page 30, bottom right)*. Then continue shaking until one or more sticks fall out. If a whole mass of them fall out – more than three, say – put them back and start again. Ideally, you just want one stick, but two or even three can be read at one time. The order does not matter.

Once you have shaken out a stick (or two, or three), read the number painted down the side. This will give you the reference number for the particular poem. So, for example, if stick 15 falls out, you then turn to poem 15 and read the divination given there, plus the traditional interpretation and the commentary, or reflection. If sticks 15 and 29 have fallen out, read the commentaries for both and see whether together they cast further light on your question.

Some Examples

Let us say that the question has been: 'Should I finish my relationship with X and start a new relationship with Y?' The divination stick that falls out is number 37. The poem says:

A great scholar knows the laws of Nature,
Seeing that as you sow, so shall you also reap.
There is no use praying to Heaven for your sins.
You will only find redemption in righteous living.

This is a powerful voice telling you that you know what is right. Do it. The traditional explanation says, in effect, deal with the issues that are distressing you now and do so with kindness; this is not an easy time, but it will pass. The commentary says: look away from just your own concerns and see the needs of others. You need to look to others' needs first and then to your own.

This strongly hints at not breaking off your relationship unless it really is a case of it being a greater kindness to the one you are leaving. It emphasizes that you are not the only person (or even the most important person) in this crisis. You need to look beyond yourself and to consider others and righteous living first and foremost.

Let us now consider what happens where you get two readings. This time the question is: 'Should I change the direction of my career and seek something new?'

Here, you get divination sticks 12 and 61. The poems read as follows:

Fortune changes quickly, both good and ill.
The bad times end, good luck will come again,
Find the wise man living on the mountain,
And his kind words will turn your life around.

The oracle is ambiguous; who can read it?
To some it means rebel and you will succeed.
But the honest general read it otherwise,
And found to his cost that this meaning was true.

Both poems are telling you to seriously consider changing. They are also honest about the difficulties you will experience, and they advise seeking professional and wise advice from someone outside your own situation. Essentially the poems recommend change.

The traditional interpretations are also clear – that, while it is risky, change is good. However, you are advised not simply to throw your old life away, but to invest wisely and not to try to travel too far away.

The reflection says this will be a hard decision, but you need to find someone who can offer you a wider, deeper, and more spiritual understanding of what you could do. Do not dodge this change, but be aware of what a change it will be.

THE THREE SECTIONS OF EACH DIVINATION

Original Poem

This first part is the original divination poem. Some of these poems were written down more than six hundred years ago by poets who were devotees of the particular deity and who are believed to have been inspired by that deity. The most famous of these are the ones for Kuan Yin, written down around AD 1450 from collections of poems left at her major shrines and temples. Some have been given in trances, such as the poems of Immortal Wong Tai, written on sand by someone filled with the spirit of the deity. Others have grown through the centuries from poems, successful divinations, inspiration, and revelation, such as those of the Jade Emperor. Yet others arise from the vast literature inspired by a deity, such as those of Kuan Ti or from a local form or version of a major deity such as Cheng Huang. In a sense they all share one origin. The Voice of the Tao constantly reminds us that we are part of something bigger, deeper, wider, and more wonderful than we usually think.

Traditional Interpretation

The second part of the divination is the traditional interpretation. Many people find it enough simply to read the poem and allow it to speak to them at whatever level is appropriate. But others have always wanted to have some further explanation or interpretation. This second reading, therefore, is a distillation of this traditional wisdom of interpretation given by professional fortune-tellers and in the complex handbooks of divination.

Reflection

This third part is new. The imagery of the poems or the historical events alluded to in the poems may be obscure to Western readers, so it has been created with them in mind. This commentary also links the profound insights of the Chinese tradition with insights from other cultures, faiths and beliefs, as well as speaking to the Western way of thinking. It is designed to act as a bridge between worlds, as well as a way into the deeper meaning of some of the images, symbols, and history shaping the poems.

AFTER THE READING

Once you have found your reading, return to it over the next day or two. Do not rush into decisions, but allow time for you to absorb its meaning and for it to become part of you. Then, and only then, should you make your mind up. And always remember that there are specialists out there who can help you deal with medical and emotional issues. If the reading gives you a better understanding of what is happening, then go and talk to the experts, who will help to sort out the practical consequences of your new understanding. Do not expect the sticks to sort out the problems themselves.

FIND YOUR ROOTS

Finally, if you are a believer in any faith, seek the guidance of your own faith. Open your own holy books – even if you have ignored them for years. Read and ponder. Think about what you believe to be the Ultimate Force of the Universe, God, Allah, Krishna or whoever. Hear them through the voice of the reading, and wonder what your god says to you. You are surrounded by traditions and beliefs as great as those of the Chinese. Draw upon them as well as upon this book.

THE DIVINATION POEMS

The sixty-four divination poems and interpretations are included on the following pages. Remember that they can only offer *guidance* – they cannot *tell* you what to do. The decisions you make are, ultimately, up to you.

1

The Han dynasty began with the fall of a great city;
Two generals strove to be the conqueror,
One threw up walls around it, but the mightiest
Could break them down to claim his throne.

TRADITIONAL INTERPRETATION

Just as the general in this story became an Emperor, this predicts that you will rise to a high position, so long as you seize the opportunities given to you and strike while the iron is hot. In particular, this is a very good fortune for anything to do with business affairs, although it is possible you will have difficulties with a particularly tenacious rival. It is also a fortunate moment for you to commit yourself to any kind of relationship, and existing relationships will grow stronger.

REFLECTION

The symbol of the fall of a great city means that, in what you are about to do, you must think big. The odds may seem stacked against you, but in reality the time is right. Yes, you will meet opposition but this should not deter you. In particular, if those who oppose you are guilty of oppression or abuse of power, then the need to overcome them is greater.

The dead trees break into green once more;
The woods are alive with buzzing life.
The immortal peach tree gives forth its fruit,
And all the lost find their way home.

TRADITIONAL INTERPRETATION

In this verse, winter turns to spring, and new life is born. Your own affairs will prosper in time, given the natural course of things. All you need to do is let Nature take its course – opportunities will naturally come your way, especially with a little self-discipline. Though your gains will not be great, they will come steadily and certainly, whether in business or in personal relationships. Prosperity is just a matter of time.

REFLECTION

This is a vision of wonder and joy – not just because spring is on the way, but because the immortal peaches are ripe. This only happens once every thousand years. All the signs suggest that this is a most auspicious time.

三

The mother sparrow builds with clay against a storm,
The traveller struggles against the driving rain,
Her fledglings huddle inside the nest,
But the clay melts and falls – all efforts futile.

TRADITIONAL INTERPRETATION

Your current precautions against disaster are unlikely to be of any use. Rather than wearing yourself out trying to defend against all possible calamities, concentrate on the good aspects of your life. With care and consideration you can build these up, so that when bad times do come you are easily able to weather them. Paying attention to your finances is wise, as is cautious investment in long-term projects. This is a good time to travel and meet new people, but do not commit yourself to somebody personally unless you are very sure you can trust them.

REFLECTION

All the imagery here is of struggle, anxiety, and difficulties. In the midst of this, do not give up. Continue to plan, to build, to try to journey on, even if all collapses or seems to do so. The mother's love never ceases, nor can the traveller act as if he or she is not travelling. It is difficult, but not beyond hope. Keep going, and eventually all will be better.

The hero was stronger than two bulls.
He could cross three rivers in one leap.
But all his strength was of no use
Against false claims by evil men.

四

TRADITIONAL INTERPRETATION

You should try to be content with what you have rather than overreaching yourself. Although you may be very competent at your work, you are likely not paying enough attention to your home life. At the moment, high positions are beyond your reach. Avoid getting involved in disputes with others, particularly within the family, and postpone travel unless strictly necessary because it will involve many delays and harassments.

REFLECTION

The sheer destructiveness of those who gossip, who attack those they envy, by chipping away at their good name, is condemned here, but it is also feared. If you are under attack by those around you through unkind words or petty actions, this can wear you out and cause you great distress. You may feel you should not be affected by such silly things. But this poem tells you that you are not alone in feeling this way. Even the strongest can be reduced to tears and unhappiness by those who maliciously attack or criticize them. Keep going, and you will recover.

5

五

A gale tore apart the garden's flowers,
Leaving only broken plants in every bed.
Kind folk took pity upon the shattered lawn,
Planting new seeds for its rebirth.

TRADITIONAL INTERPRETATION

Be cautious in your plans because they can easily go wrong at this point. Disaster lurks just around the corner, but can be avoided with forethought and discretion. Your personal relationships may be difficult for a while, and you may have business difficulties, but your friends will eventually come through for you. Take care over details, particularly in selecting medical treatment or planning a journey.

REFLECTION

Gardening was one of the great arts of China – a visible attempt by humanity to impose order without destroying the overarching order of the Tao (Nature). This image reminds us that even the most lovely of things, done for the best of reasons, can be destroyed by the very forces we are trying to work with. But the image goes on to show that after such a disaster you must start again. Do not give in – you have to carry on.

Live in the wilderness with only the ravens as friends,
Know yourself and do not envy others' wealth.
Everybody's capable of finding their own bread,
But nobody gets to see the whole world.

六

TRADITIONAL INTERPRETATION

You should try to live your life in accordance with Nature and count your blessings rather than envying others. Material goods may be scarce for a while, but your friends and family may well be able to support you both emotionally and financially. You should invest money in long-term businesses now, but you may suffer some financial losses along the way. Equally, if you have a medical problem you should try to get it treated immediately. People and objects you thought were lost will turn up soon.

REFLECTION

This calls to mind the prophet Elijah in the Bible, who fled from the persecution of the enemies of God and lived in the desert, his food being brought by ravens. Both that story and this poem remind us that, while we may strive for much, sometimes we need to be content with what we have. We may want the world but should learn to find true value in the ordinary – as the Christian mystic Mother Julian of Norwich did when she realized that the whole universe was contained in a walnut.

7

七

Although he reached a great position,
Wise Lu did not care for earthly things.
He brewed instead the pills of heaven,
Forging immortality in his earthly crucible.

TRADITIONAL INTERPRETATION

This is an extremely good fortune. Your position in life should soon improve, and great wealth is potentially at hand. Any plans you're acting on at the moment are likely to be successful and lead to high prospects. If you are ill, you will soon recover with proper treatment. Visitors from overseas are likely, and your personal relationships will be happy and content.

REFLECTION

Power comes in two forms. There is temporal power – being head of your group, the big boss, able to throw your weight around. But those who understand real power look to the second kind – spiritual power. This power does not seek to dominate, but to become so fully at one with the Tao that you never die, living forever in its ebb and flow. Immortality is ultimate union with the Tao and is the greatest symbol of true power, attainable only if you use this life – the earthly crucible – to help and care for as many as you can.

The turtle dove invades the home of the magpie,
Leaving one a thief, one homeless, both discontent.
When plants of different natures twist together,
Nobody can possibly tell what they hide.

TRADITIONAL INTERPRETATION

This fortune suggests that, unless you change your ways, you are likely to bring only disharmony and trouble for yourself and others. Unless you take great care in what you say, you are likely to be the target of harmful gossip. You should be extremely careful about your health, and it would be unwise to make any new business decisions. Travelling is undesirable, and you have little chance of financial success in the immediate future.

REFLECTION

This poem is a warning. Do not mix together that which Nature keeps separate. The turtle dove and the magpie are birds whose symbolism in China could not be more different. To bring them together like this is nonsensical to the Chinese. The poem says that whatever or whoever you are caught up with, in ways that are unnatural or wrong, will only bring you grief. Go your separate ways, or if you stay together be honest about the problems this will bring.

9

九

Why bother with the pains of hate and greed?
Just as the full moon lights up the traveller's path,
So too can your conscience guide your life.
Let your heart be like that moon: full, bright and clear.

TRADITIONAL INTERPRETATION

The full moon in this fortune represents hope for the future. Though things may seem confused at the moment, if you follow your conscience, everything will become clear. You need to make a clear division between right and wrong in your life. If you do this, it will be a good time for you. Your newfound clarity will benefit both your personal life and your business. The relationship with your family, particularly with your parents, will improve.

REFLECTION

You know what is right and what is wrong. Stop pretending otherwise. All may seem obscure and troubling around you, but let your conscience dictate, and you will find the right path to follow.

Disease afflicts all folk alike,
No matter how upright their conduct.
Even a faithful student of Confucius
Became a leper and died alone.

TRADITIONAL INTERPRETATION

Although your personal conduct is good, troubles may lie ahead. Your personal reputation is in jeopardy, and you should be aware that others may be spreading rumors about you. Unless you are careful and restrained, you may be faced with many creditors and lawsuits. This is not a good time to start new projects; instead, you should try to defend what you already have.

REFLECTION

The story of the Confucian student who died sick and alone is well-known in China. Sickness was often seen as a judgment meted out by the deities to those who had done wrong. But what 'wrong' had the student of Confucius done? This is rather like the Book of Job in the Bible which asks 'Why?' to the issue of sickness and disaster. Ultimately this poem reminds us that wealth, power, and fame are meaningless to disease. In the end, we are all but human and weak.

十二

The trees form a green curtain by the river.
I sleep in their shade in summer, when the light is long,
Watching the swallows take their playful path by,
Among the gentle breezes and hanging trees.

TRADITIONAL INTERPRETATION

If you concentrate on your home life rather than your work, this can be a very prosperous time for you. You need not worry too much about your work because things will probably turn out well whatever you do. Truly good fortune, however, will come through your family and friends. This is a very fertile time: if you want children you will probably have them, and any investments or land you own will give a very good return.

REFLECTION

Delight in what is around you! Enjoy the ordinariness of what you have. Do not go looking for great wonders or marvels in foreign lands or with exotic people. Where you are, there is already more than enough to enjoy, wonder at, and discover. Stay put, and discover the extraordinary.

Fortune changes quickly, both good and ill.
The bad times end, good luck will come again.
Find the wise man living on the mountain,
And his kind words will turn your life around.

十二

TRADITIONAL INTERPRETATION

You may be going through a brief period of misfortune at the moment, but things will soon turn around with the aid of another. You will have enough money to provide not only the basic necessities of life, but plenty of little luxuries as well. You should put any money that comes to you into long-term investments rather than spending it immediately. This is not a good time to travel, as you will have many problems and may be late in returning to your home.

REFLECTION

The Chinese character for an immortal, a great sage, is made up of two other characters – that for a human alone and that for a mountain. The sage is the person who lives alone on the mountain, shunning human politics and society. To be encouraged to go and see such a person means that you need to put your life into a wider, more profound perspective. You are probably far too caught up in material things and need to recover the spiritual.

十三

Grandfather Kiang fished all day,
Though once a minister, he'd put such things away.
But when the country needed him again,
He ceased his fishing to ease the country's pain.

TRADITIONAL INTERPRETATION

The time is not ripe for whatever plans you have at present and you should wait a while before putting them into effect. It is better at the moment to remain inactive and enjoy your hobbies, but wealth and status are in store in the future. It may take you some time to recover from any current health problems, but legal difficulties should soon clear up. Somebody important to you who is currently absent will return soon.

REFLECTION

This poem is about duty. It cites the famous case of a wise official who longed for the peace and quiet of retirement but who, when duty called, took up the burden of high office and responsibility again. There are things you have to do, responsibilities you must fulfill. It is no good trying to leave them to others or pretending that it is not up to you, because it is.

The hermit delights in the rain on his roof,
Beating its pattern against his woven thatch.
He drinks himself to sleep among the apricots,
And hates the wakeful chatter of the birds.

十四

TRADITIONAL INTERPRETATION

Your prospects are good, but not wonderful. Any chance of money will certainly be delayed for some time, but you should think about other matters. Your family life will be much as normal, but also be cautious of what others may be saying about you. Any improvement in your life will likely be gradual and come with new problems. Though these difficulties may bother you, remember that nothing is perfect in this world.

REFLECTION

The hermit is a strange person in Chinese legend. He often lives quite a raucous life, enjoying alcohol especially! Apricots are a symbol of long life. This poem uses the imagery of the hermit, alcohol, apricots, and a rude awakening to say that self-indulgence may be all right for a while, but if you really seek a long life you must wake up to the harsher realities surrounding you.

十五

The hillwalker faints from the heat of the sun,
So Nature's curse will soon strike you down too.
Like a bird driven by predators from its nest,
You'll only find solace in the depths of the forest.

TRADITIONAL INTERPRETATION

As a bird seeks shelter in the forest, you will encounter hardship and troubles at first, but all your troubles will eventually be over. Do not seek revenge on people who have hurt you, nor should you attempt false reconciliations; simply live and let live. Be cautious about your personal safety, as there is a chance of an accident. Existing relationships will grow stronger, but few new ones are likely to be formed soon. Your work will go well, and you may be offered a promotion.

REFLECTION

Troubles have come upon you. Perhaps you have overstretched yourself or have been unlucky. Your ordinary, settled way of life has been turned upside down. Do not pretend this is not happening. It is. What you need to do is learn from this. Go deep within yourself, go deep within your own faith, and find at the center of your own dark forest the strength to recover, to learn, and to start again. It is there.

十六

Though his stepmother slandered him to his father's face,
The faithful son loved her despite all her faults.
When her illness had brought her near the gate of death,
He found her medicine and warmed her heart forever.

TRADITIONAL INTERPRETATION

Any divisions in your life at the moment will require a lot of time and effort to settle, but this is not too large a price to pay for peace, as the consequences of letting disagreements continue could be horrendous. Your chances of personal gain are slim and your health uncertain, but you can work to help others. Place other people before yourself, and their gratitude will make your life much easier.

REFLECTION

The famous legend of Shun the Filial, whose father left him to the attacks of his new wife and her family, is one of the classics of Confucian piety. The moral of the story of selfless obedience to the rules of filial piety was that the Emperor Yao heard of this and appointed Shun to be his successor. Troubles borne bravely now will bring rewards in the future.

The river's reeds are tipped with morning dew,
Moonlight bathes the stone courtyard steps.
I hear the neigh of horses on the soft breeze,
Swiftly following the bell's call to rise.

TRADITIONAL INTERPRETATION

While you have a decent chance of being both respected and admired for your actions, wealth will not necessarily accompany this. It is time to make firm decisions about your relationships: either committing yourself definitely or breaking away for good. In general, your life will progress fairly smoothly without major upsets. If you feel depressed, you should start thinking about helping other people rather than yourself.

REFLECTION

The most beautiful time of day is early in the morning, exquisitely recalled in this poem. But there is another meaning. So the story goes, a young servant, up early in order to enjoy the morning air and ready to work, heard upon the wind the faint sound of enemy soldiers approaching on horseback to attack the palace. He raised the alarm just in time. Be alert. Be ready. You have no idea when the peace and quiet will be broken by changing events.

Far off the raven falls and the rabbit rises,
So things have been since the start of time.
Believe in Buddha and the Tao and you will find wisdom,
Whether you are scholar or peasant, worker or merchant.

TRADITIONAL INTERPRETATION

The setting and rising of the sun (the raven) and the moon (the rabbit) symbolizes the ups and downs of human life. Harmony between the two is a sign of good fortune, and you should seek a similar harmony in your own life. If you manage this, everything will be secure and successful. Attempt to remain calm and look to understand your enemies rather than opposing them directly. If you have any firm plans for the future, you should start putting them into effect now. Maybe now is a good time to think about moving.

REFLECTION

Yin and yang are at the heart of this poem. The raven, symbol of the sun, is yang. The rabbit, symbol of the moon, is yin. Buddha, busy teaching and organizing, is yang. The Tao, calm and just being, is yin. You too are both yin and yang: you need the energy of the yang to be balanced by the yin of calmness. Look to yourself. If the balance is not quite right, learn to cultivate it in order that you can achieve essential harmony.

19

十九

On the kitchen floor the kitten lies,
Lazily warming herself in the afternoon sun.
Graceful animals always bring good luck,
And should be protected whenever possible.

TRADITIONAL INTERPRETATION

This is a very good fortune, and it predicts great luck in anything you do. Your best path to happiness, however, is through romance: you will only ultimately find yourself by looking in another. Do not allow apparent obstacles to deter you – remember that love eventually finds a way. Foreign travel will probably be extremely successful.

REFLECTION

The imagery here echoes an older poem in which a lovesick soldier on duty in the cold north recalls his lover's kitten, relaxed, warm, and content in her house in the south. In his mind he travels to be with her. This poem says you should appreciate what you have and, if you leave it, treasure it and seek to be reunited as soon as possible. You may be striving to achieve great things, but really you would like to be your beloved's cat!

All names in Heaven are unique,
And even earthly things cannot be the same.
Your future is set within the Book of Fate,
Which never confuses praise and blame.

二十

TRADITIONAL INTERPRETATION

Although your fate is partially predetermined, your own actions can alter your destiny. Good deeds, especially those which genuinely cost you time and effort, and particularly any that involve travelling, will rebound to your benefit. Your future prosperity depends upon your own kindness. Be careful about your family's safety as well. Your personal relationships will remain in a state of flux for some time.

REFLECTION

You are both determined by fate and have your future within your own hands! Chinese belief says certain things are fixed - such as when you are born, where, and into what sort of a family – and beyond that everything else is in your power to change. Your fortune should not be confused by the things people around you say or suggest. Act with integrity in all that you do, and do not be swayed by praise or hints of glory.

Marriage is a blessed union indeed,
When done in accordance with yin and yang.
The dragon and the phoenix coil together,
Uniting in a sweet dream of love.

TRADITIONAL INTERPRETATION

This fortune describes the harmony of the universe, with the dragon and phoenix representing yang and yin respectively. It prophesies good fortune, especially in love. If you are currently single, you will probably find a new partner soon, and existing relationships will be strengthened. In general, everything will go harmoniously for you, and your own health and safety – if you maintain the right balance of yin and yang in your life – is guaranteed.

REFLECTION

All things will work out positively. Yin and yang are the basic building blocks of the universe and, when in balance, all goes well. You need to find someone who will complement you, bring a sense of balance and harmony to your life. Forget excitement and danger: you need someone who can offer you what is missing from the dynamics of your life. It is for you to work out whether that is yin or yang!

22

The drunken poet wrote of wine and love.
His Emperor, Ming, loved verse and song.
When they were introduced, they found
Mutual friendship in the balm of poetry.

二十二

TRADITIONAL INTERPRETATION

This is an excellent fortune, predicting great opportunities for you, both personally and professionally. Soon you will have the chance to form a new friendship, providing you with the emotional support you may be missing currently. Problems, especially legal ones, will resolve themselves naturally if you do not create more troubles for yourself. Your social and financial position may soon improve, and your family and close friends may also prosper as a result of your newfound wealth.

REFLECTION

This delightful image – of the laid-back drunken Taoist poet and the hard-working Confucian Emperor finding solace in each other's company – has a simple message: do not reject or turn away from those who at first glance seem totally different from you. It may just be that you are both what the other needs. Take time to find out. Do not judge too hastily.

23

二十三

Health, fortune, fame – they are all illusion.
Prosperity is only a game played by fools.
The fruit of success tastes sour in the mouth.
Soon you will mourn your dreams of worldly glory.

TRADITIONAL INTERPRETATION

You are surrounded by illusions, and many concealed dangers await you. While your future prospects may appear good, this may not really be the case. You should consider any seeming chance to make extra money extremely carefully, as it could be a trick. Equally, somebody in your personal life may be deceiving you, especially about children. Hidden ailments might be troubling you physically, and you should try to get a thorough medical checkup soon.

REFLECTION

This could hardly be clearer. The things you currently value most – the material aspects of your life – are not what is really valuable. Indeed, they are traps. Look very deep within, and see what truly lies there.

Life is broken by meaningless quarrels,
Like fallen blossoms drifting over the ocean.
You will never find grace behaving like a fool.
All that can leave you is a heap of troubles.

二十四

TRADITIONAL INTERPRETATION

Troubles lurk ahead, but you have no option but to put up with your present difficulties. Remember that tolerance can be a lifesaver, and avoid talking about others behind their back. Look after everything carefully and avoid risks; just keep on working as hard as possible. Only your own determination and willpower can bear you through the problems that are coming, though it may be a good idea to move to a new area if your problems seem totally insurmountable.

REFLECTION

Something is keeping you from resolving a profound problem. The Bible says never to let the sun go down on your anger. Resolve differences quickly; otherwise they embitter you, twist you up, and waste your energies, as well as of those of the person you are angry with. In the end, disagreements must be solved – unless, of course, you want to ruin everything you have worked for.

Emperor Ming slew his one true love,
But a shaman took pity and eased his heart,
With dreams of roaming upon the moon,
His beloved mistress forever at his side.

TRADITIONAL INTERPRETATION

While you seem to have suffered a great loss at the moment, some kind of reconciliation will occur, although it may only be a partial and unfulfilling one. Things will set themselves right but not for a while. Your professional prospects are better than your personal ones, so it may be a good idea to take some time off work to attend to your private life. Maybe you have been neglecting the spiritual side of your personality.

REFLECTION

What is gone is gone and you must now learn to live with that. Recall and enjoy the best of what was, but also move on. You will never get over what has happened because it is now part of you, but this can strengthen and guide you rather than hang around your neck like some sort of curse.

26

二十六

The shadows of flowers hang about the doorposts,
And the moon reflects the traveller's weary face.
A crane's mournful cry breaks the silent night,
Urging the wanderer to hurry back to his home.

TRADITIONAL INTERPRETATION

When you embark on any endeavor, you should look out for warning signs that the enterprise may not be as successful as you hoped. If you find any such clues, cut your losses as soon as possible. Do not waste your energy in useless persistence, and remember that good times cannot last forever. For you, success in anything depends on both choosing the right moment and ensuring that you have a safe refuge if things go badly.

REFLECTION

The good times do not last! You have had it good for some time, but look for the signs of inevitable change and decay. There is nothing to be afraid of in this. Change is inevitable, as the I-Ching always reminds us. The Buddha saw dependency on what is bound to change as one of the main causes of human misery. And Jesus said to live each day as if it were your last. So watch for the shadows of change, and welcome them as you would the cool of autumn after the heat of summer.

27

Your plans are carefully constructed,
But fear stops you from completing them.
When the time is right, a noble patron
Will help you establish a comfortable home.

TRADITIONAL INTERPRETATION

Your life is like a peaceful and wealthy mansion defended by a strong fence. You can enjoy peace and prosperity safely, and both you and your family are largely free from danger. If you try to make more money quickly, though, you will find difficulties, and you should make long-term investments instead. Existing problems will drag out for some time, but will turn out all right in the end. For instance, illnesses will most likely be prolonged but have no lasting effects.

REFLECTION

You have everything planned, but somehow you cannot ever let yourself go and thus do what you keep planning. To do so you may need to seek help from someone who can stand back from the issues and cast a calm, detached eye over your plans. Look for such a person, and listen to their advice. If it seems sound, do not hesitate.

The scholar made a pledge on the bridge,
Saying 'I shall not cross here again,
Unless I come in a horse-drawn carriage.'
Fortune blessed him; he crossed the bridge again.

二十八

TRADITIONAL INTERPRETATION

You cannot achieve all your goals immediately. Be patient: wealth and status take both effort and time to achieve, but eventually the trappings of prosperity will be yours. You should work on personal relationships before committing yourself permanently to them. While business problems will soon be resolved, your health may be bad for some time.

REFLECTION

A scholar in China had many opportunities for success once he passed the Imperial exams, for honor and lucrative appointments lay that way. But to achieve this he had to devote himself to study every day and for many years. It was usually worth it. Take time – you must work for what you want, not just assume it is yours by right.

Fish on my plate; flowers by my side.
I enjoy the cool evening with a sip of fine wine.
The tide is rising; the boat is moving.
My heart is joyous; my spirit is high.

TRADITIONAL INTERPRETATION

This fortune depicts a man enjoying the pleasures of late summer and waiting for the move into a gentle autumn. Like him, you should delight in the diversions available to you now, and not worry yourself about future problems, as good luck and well-being are largely assured. Your hopes and dreams will eventually realize themselves, and you only need to continue as you are to move smoothly into a pleasant and prosperous season of your life.

REFLECTION

Be at peace. You have worked hard, and now it is time to rest. Your fiery, energetic yang nature has been dominant. Now it is time for your quieter, calmer, and more reflective yin nature to take over. You need to rest if you wish to enjoy what you have gained and to sample again the simple delights of life.

The best thing, I tell you, is not to aim too high.
A flying stork will not see the fatal arrow.
Gathering wood, you may uncover a snake,
And you will regret forever its poisonous bite.

三十

TRADITIONAL INTERPRETATION

Be content with your lot, and restrain yourself from too high an ambition. Take precautions against possible dangers, and seal your mouth. Try to avoid getting involved in other people's quarrels. Your personal health is uncertain, and you may bring problems upon yourself by rash speech. Financially, you do not have much hope of improvement at the moment – bide your time and new prospects will come to you.

REFLECTION

The somewhat contradictory message of this poem is this: expect the unexpected. It warns that trouble comes when you least expect it. The stork, believed by the Chinese to fly higher and to live longer than any other bird, can be killed by an arrow rising up through the clouds. Disturbing things can also prove dangerous. Be watchful and careful. Do not assume you are unassailable.

31

三十一

Two scholars went to the capital for examinations;
One passed and stayed, one failed and returned
Carrying a letter from his friend. He fell ill,
But eventually – thank Heaven! – came home.

TRADITIONAL INTERPRETATION

You may be beset with worries at the moment, but your life will improve, step by step, over time. There will be no miraculous solutions to your problems but instead a gradual recovery. Old friends may soon arrive to help you, and the time is ripe to make firmer commitments in your personal life. In the long run, happiness really does lie ahead.

REFLECTION

The aim of every scholar in China was to go to the capital to take the final Imperial exam. Being successful opened the way to glory, power, and wealth. But not to pass the exam meant failure and great disappointment. This story, however, makes the following point. Although the one who failed had to return home, the strain of failure made him ill. Being ill made him realize how much he longed for the security, love, and friendship of home – even if he did not come home in triumph. Appreciate what you have.

三十二

He endured the bleak north for nineteen years,
His captured banner trailing upon the distant sands.
Snow was his only food; his heart was full of woe,
And his only companions the sheep he tended.

TRADITIONAL INTERPRETATION

This fortune refers to a famous Chinese general, Su Wu, who was taken prisoner by the northern barbarians and forced to work as a shepherd. Like him, at the moment you may seem to be in a position below your true worth. You must seek to take pride and pleasure in the work you do, rather than dreaming of past or future glories. Learn to bear adversity with good will, and you may attain the status you truly deserve.

REFLECTION

This very famous story is about steadfast loyalty. The general was captured by the Mongols, who at first tried to bribe him into betraying the Emperor. When that failed, they sent him into the wilds to guard the sheep. Yet he refused to deny his Emperor. Loyalty is what will bring you through. Do not be tempted by easy solutions, nor expect that things will go smoothly. Stay the course, and you will have done the right thing.

三十三

You do not see the valuables within your grasp,
So you turn around and around in a vain search.
Relax and wait for the arrival of another,
For they can tell you where the treasure is hidden.

TRADITIONAL INTERPRETATION

Better prospects are much closer than you realize, and fortune will aid you in finding them, so you do not need to spend so much time looking for new opportunities yourself. Personally, you have very little to worry about, and your family will also be blessed with good luck if you take the time to care for them. It is not a good time to move against others, to travel, or to invest in risky enterprises – maintain your current position instead.

REFLECTION

Sometimes we are too close to things to see their true value. We become myopic. So we spend time looking for what we already have, searching for that which is not lost.

He was a great commander, but ugly and squat,
And so found himself rejected by two mighty kings.
But a high official saw his value, beneath his scars,
Sought him through the night and won his aid.

TRADITIONAL INTERPRETATION

Do not judge by appearances, or you may overlook great resources and opportunities. Instead, investigate things closely before making any judgment, especially in legal situations. Unless you are careful, your current affluence may slip away from you. Do not believe the rumors you hear about others: remember that people may be spreading similar stories about you.

REFLECTION

The meaning of this poem is clear, and a frequent insight in divination poems. Do not judge by outward appearances, for to find a beautiful piece of jade you first have to break open a plain piece of rock. Beware also of being condescending. The high official had to work to undo the damage done to the ugly commander, who later became the God of Literature's chief attendant. Value everyone as an equal.

When Heaven chooses a man for greatness,
It first makes him suffer terribly in body and soul.
Happiness does not come to anyone easily.
There is always a good reason for wealth or poverty.

TRADITIONAL INTERPRETATION

As this fortune says, you will not achieve anything without experiencing a fair amount of worry and suffering along the way. Be careful and discriminating before embarking on a new scheme, but throw all your efforts into whatever you eventually decide to do. Do not be dissuaded by the difficulties you encounter, as you will win through in the end. Try to anticipate problems before they occur so you are prepared to deal with them. Try your best to reconcile yourself with any friends or family you are currently estranged from, and do not be afraid to commit yourself to a relationship.

REFLECTION

Too often we assume today that we have a right to be happy, that nothing is worth struggling for. We assume that if we are not enjoying ourselves we should move on and abandon relationships or situations. But this belief in happiness is so damaging for it leads us to give up before we have even started. You must persevere. The struggle is necessary for a sense of true worth to arise. Stick with it and you will find, perhaps not happiness exactly, but something even better – contentment.

You are ill and caught up in problems, but be calm.
Many benefits and riches are waiting for you still.
A clever monkey can loose himself from a golden chain,
And roam about freely in his mountain home.

三十六

TRADITIONAL INTERPRETATION

Like the monkey the fortune describes, you will be able to free yourself from your current problems, provided you are cunning. Once these problems are over, very little will be beyond your reach. People close to you may have an uncertain time for a while, but your own prosperity is virtually assured. Look for the lost (be they people or objects) far away from where you are now.

REFLECTION

The image of the monkey on a golden chain is a favorite one in China, used to express a conundrum. The pet monkey has all it needs by way of food, drink, and luxury – hence the gold chain. But it does not have freedom. The sage Chuang Tzu was once asked to become a minister in the Emperor's court. He refused, saying he would feel like the sacrificed bull, which is well-fed but destined for destruction. He wanted to remain free. Are you trapped in a world of goods that is like a golden chain around your neck?

A great scholar knows the laws of Nature,
Seeing that as you sow, so shall you also reap.
There is no use praying to Heaven for your sins.
You will only find redemption in righteous living.

TRADITIONAL INTERPRETATION

Words are of no use without deeds to accompany them. You should try to settle the problems you have now, and (as always) kind deeds are the best way to assure a good fortune. Wealth and status are beyond your reach at the moment, but personal relationships are more favored by fate. Sickness will only pass if you seek some medical assistance.

REFLECTION

This poem seems to echo the words of Jesus. Not only did He say you reap what you sow, but He also said that those who simply prayed would not enter Heaven; only those who cared for the sick, the poor, those in prison, for example, would get there. This poem says the same. Forget religious practices and rituals, meditation or crystal gazing. Unless you live a life of service to others, how can you expect Heaven's favors?

Free from his day's work, the poet sailed leisurely home.
Though not spacious, his little cottage always served him well.
He would write poems or drink wine by the south window,
Or go for a lazy stroll, enjoying the beauty of the mountains.

三十八

TRADITIONAL INTERPRETATION

While you are unlikely to achieve great fame, you will probably find happiness, provided you are prepared to settle for modest gains rather than overreaching yourself. You should learn to avoid taking risks and exercise caution in most matters. Little effort is required on your part for you to achieve a contented life.

REFLECTION

Contentment is the theme of this poem. We see poets as creatures of leisure. But most Chinese poets were scholars, administrators, or judges. They worked hard, but when the day was done – or they had retired – they found true peace in being content with the simple things of life.

39

The message has come from a far distant horizon.
Its meaning is obscure – just worthless nonsense.
You cannot turn a stone into a polished mirror;
So do not waste your time, save your labour instead.

TRADITIONAL INTERPRETATION

You are being foolish in attempting things beyond your ability. Although you craft a thousand schemes, all of them will probably fail. Opt for patience rather than rashness, and try to be content with your lot. Be careful of your own safety, as a serious accident may occur soon. This is not a good time to commit to relationships – let things cool off for awhile, and think about them calmly.

REFLECTION

The image of trying to polish a stone in order to make a mirror is very common in China. Traditional mirrors were made by polishing brass or copper, but, whereas these can be brought to such perfection as to afford a reflection, an ordinary stone cannot. So with you as well. Do not expend time and energy trying to make one thing into something it cannot ever be. Allow each to be true to its own innate nature, as Chuang Tzu the sage so often said. To force one thing to become what it is not is to fail twice.

四十

The countryside was full of chaos and disorder,
Before the new Emperor came with the Mandate of Heaven.
A good ruler serves the whole country, both poor and rich,
And brings peace, prosperity and good times for all.

TRADITIONAL INTERPRETATION

An extremely good fortune presaging the likely attainment of many of your goals. Fate will probably shield you against most illnesses and accidents and, if you work hard and help others, you will find joy in everything you do. You should consider settling down permanently and committing yourself to your partner, as relationships sealed now are likely to be very successful.

REFLECTION

The Mandate of Heaven means the right to rule. Chinese emperors were called the Sons of Heaven. If chaos, war, civil unrest, bad harvests, and adverse weather conditions afflicted the State, this was seen as a clear sign that Heaven had withdrawn the right to rule from the Imperial family. See the present times of disturbance as the passing of an old corrupt way, and be prepared to look for the new way, the new order, which will restore order because it has been blessed.

41

四十一

In the moonlight the boat floated among the stars,
Bringing together lovers that fate has set apart.
For her love he became a distant planet.
Nobody knows how much he has suffered.

TRADITIONAL INTERPRETATION

It is time to look around for chances for profit, friendship, or romance. While an element of deceit may be involved, you are likely to form strong new bonds soon. Your plans will be realized, provided you are prepared to work hard for them. Physically, you will likely remain fit and healthy, but somebody close to you may fall ill. Visitors are likely to arrive soon, probably with good news.

REFLECTION

Stories of ill-fated lovers turned into stars that are allowed to meet occasionally are great favorites in China. The moral is that some loves are fated not to be fulfilled, but that love is nevertheless of boundless worth. It may be that fate frustrates your plans, but still hold true to that which you have glimpsed.

Earthly rulers bestow many blessings,
Both honourable and without any shame.
So have you been blessed by Heaven's favour,
Making your life a Paradise on earth.

TRADITIONAL INTERPRETATION

You are extremely privileged to receive the favor of Heaven, but you should be careful lest your deeds turn fate against you. Show your gratitude through good works and prayer; remember your obligations to others. Follow this advice and everything will go your way, but you should not expect great wealth. You should take care of your health during the summer.

REFLECTION

This says that sometimes the most wonderful things happen for no apparent reason. They are gifts from Heaven, a blessing, a sign of grace. Do not try to work out why – just be joyful that such events occur. Do not feel you always have to 'earn' everything. Some things simply come from the bounty of Heaven.

The prince went to a great banquet,
Fearing traitors' knives at any moment.
Abandoning pride, he sneaked away,
Saving himself to assume the throne.

TRADITIONAL INTERPRETATION

Discretion is often the better part of valor, and you should try to avoid risks now, as they may turn out to be more dangerous than you think. With caution, you can rise to high status, but you will have to travel far to find romance. You should not have any difficulties in business, and legal problems are likely to be resolved your way.

REFLECTION

Wisdom is often more useful than boastful valor. If you suspect all is not well, listen to your heart, and take suitable action. Do not be foolhardy, confronting where wisdom would tell you to walk away. If your senses warn you to beware, then listen to them.

Competing fiercely to become spring's queen,
The garden flowers blossom to their full beauty.
Who will win the golden crown of glory?
Among them all, only the peony stands out.

四十四

TRADITIONAL INTERPRETATION

Your attempts to gain wealth and fame are likely to be successful, and your personal relationships will turn out well. You need only search to find many opportunities for advancement. Do not hesitate to put your plans into operation, and it is a good idea to commit yourself more strongly to your current relationships. With care, you can remain both physically and mentally fit.

REFLECTION

The peony is the beloved flower of Chinese poets and artists, for it has a strong sexual overtone, being (in its elongated bud stage) the example par excellence of the male member and the yang principle. But its multitude of opening petals is the symbol of the female, of sex, and of the yin principle. Thus it combines the yin and yang symbolism. It is saying: be complete, both yin and yang, and you will be able to progress. Do not rely on just one aspect of your personality, nor should you be too modest. In Chinese slang, a peony is a stunningly beautiful and sexy young woman. Do not hide your light under a bushel! If you have skills and attributes, use them, show them to others, and they will appreciate you and help you to advance.

The meek will overcome the violent;
The kind-hearted will receive infinite rewards.
Their deeds of kindness bestow to such great merit,
That heavenly ambrosia will quench their thirst.

TRADITIONAL INTERPRETATION

Your best chance to gain the favor of fortune is to be kind and tender towards others. If you perform good deeds, your reputation will improve, and others will be more likely to aid you. Autumn will be your most prosperous season, although you will remain peaceful and safe throughout the year. You should be the victor in any outstanding disputes, because you are most likely in the right.

REFLECTION

The Tao Te Ching stresses how water wears away huge rocks, and the weak wears down the strong. The Taoist way is not to confront but simply to be, to flow round and under obstacles rather than try to overwhelm them. Be natural. Be considerate. Be thoughtful. Hurdles will fall, melt away, or after a while, will cease to be important.

For the sake of one child, the ruler's command
Was the death of all children in his own city.
But the orphan was hidden in a far-off state,
And, when a man, earned revenge for his father.

四十六

TRADITIONAL INTERPRETATION

This is a risky time, and you should avoid overreaching yourself. Do not get embroiled in conflicts with others, and try not to strive for wealth and fame, lest you encounter disaster along the way. You may have a tricky time in your personal life, but patience and tolerance will let you win through.

REFLECTION

Stories of special children being hunted at birth are to be found worldwide – the baby Krishna and Child Jesus are just two examples. The moral here is that rash, fearful, or vengeful actions will rebound. Trying to destroy what you fear may well lead to that fear returning a hundred times worse. In Greek legend, the basis of the tragic notion was the attempt to kill children destined to overthrow you.

47

四十七

The envoy travelled hard over a thousand miles
To claim a province for his master from another.
The king said nothing, but tears streaked his face,
Knowing he was too weak to save the province.

TRADITIONAL INTERPRETATION

Events will take a long time to be resolved and may not turn out in your favor. Periods of misfortune are likely to be particularly severe, and you will be overshadowed with worries for a good while. Committing yourself to a relationship now could be a fatal mistake. Only kind words and patience will get you through this tricky period – your friends may well be your greatest source of support.

REFLECTION

Serving faithfully one who is not able to honor your service can be seen as the highest level of loyalty... or as an act of great foolishness. It is up to you to decide. Either way, your integrity is assumed. But what outcome do you desire most of all? Remember that you always have a choice.

The humble partridge becomes the great roc;
A freedom that no other bird can know.
Higher and higher he soars into the sky,
Leaving miles of clouds far below him.

四十八

TRADITIONAL INTERPRETATION

A dramatic change is about to occur in your life – whether this is for good or bad depends on your actions. Be prepared for things to change completely, and learn to adapt with circumstances. While you may have difficulties forming new relationships, existing ones will probably be successful. Business deals will probably be delayed for some time but will prove profitable in the end.

REFLECTION

This is about contrasts. The roc was a vast, mythological creature and the partridge but a small, dull bird. Yet, says the poet, that which was humdrum and ordinary can become transformed, different. You can be in charge of your own destiny if you want to. Your actions can make you a better person. It is in your power. See if you, also, are able to change.

49

四十九

Although the general had great wisdom
And saved the Emperor's skin many a time,
He eventually fell from favour with his master,
Left the court, and escaped into oblivion.

TRADITIONAL INTERPRETATION

There are many obstacles in your way at the moment, and a complete change of lifestyle might be a good idea. You could well find happiness in ways you had never imagined; it is foolish to be complacent. Travel would be a good idea, both to get your mind off your problems and to broaden your horizons, but see if you can resolve any personal disputes before you leave.

REFLECTION

Taoism mocks fame and fortune. It sees material benefit or worldly success as little more than illusion. Taoist sages often pointed out that great heroes or model ministers frequently underwent terrible sufferings for the Empire, only to die alone or scorned. Do not invest all your energies in issues that are temporal, material, and bound to pass away. Instead, look to the things of Heaven, where your reward will be everlasting.

Fleeing a lord's wrath, the hero rushed to the river,
Where a friendly boatman ferried him over.
The hero offered him his sword in thanks, but he refused,
Placing friendship above any material reward.

五十

TRADITIONAL INTERPRETATION

While you have little to worry about, materially speaking your life is not likely to improve much for the moment. Do not work yourself too hard – learn to enjoy the pleasures of family life and your hobbies. You should take care in your business dealings and be prudent in your personal relationships. Avoid overspending, particularly around the holidays. Charitable work and good deeds will help to improve your peace of mind.

REFLECTION

This tale, taken from one of the great Chinese heroic tales, makes the point that sometimes people do things because the action is right, not out of a hope for reward. It may be that you have underestimated the support, care, and commitment of those around you. You cannot buy such things; only thank Heaven for them when you find them.

51

五十一

During the long, long summer dog days
Everybody is tortured by the burning sun.
But now a calm and soothing breeze has arisen,
The will of Heaven that eases human souls.

TRADITIONAL INTERPRETATION

At the moment, everything may seem overwhelming and your problems just too many to cope with effectively. Do not be worried – learn to relax, to avoid stress, and your problems will soon pass. Your personal life will blossom, and you are likely to make friends with someone who is in a good position to help you. Any business investments you have made, however, are likely to take a sharp downturn soon, so it would be wise to take any money now, while you still can.

REFLECTION

A hot Chinese summer can be almost unbearable. It is a small wonder, therefore, that the Emperors sacrificed to the yin spirit of cold, wet, and winter at the height of summer! But, through the rise and fall of yin and yang, summer is always followed by autumn and winter. Bear with your current situation, and you will find that things become a little easier. Change will come – it always does.

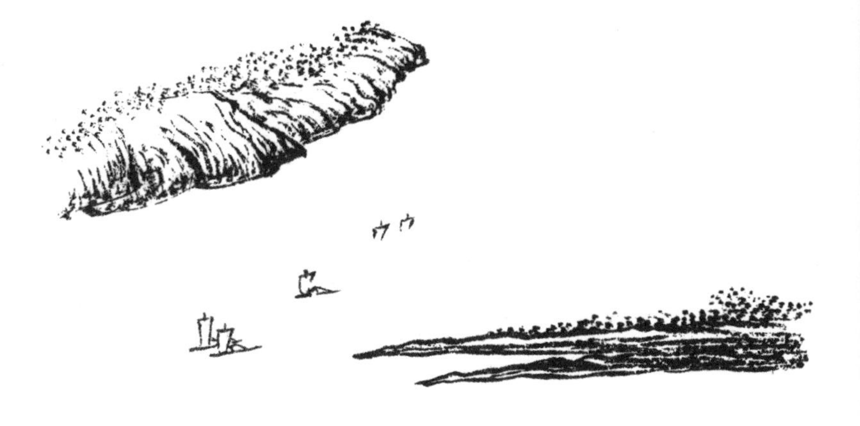

In the royal canal love poems floated on leaves,
Written by a maid in service at the court.
A scholar responded by the same means,
And at last the leaves brought the lovers together.

TRADITIONAL INTERPRETATION

While happiness awaits you, it may take many years for your current difficulties to mend. Expect a gradual recovery from your problems rather than a sudden solution. You may well find your friends are your best source of support. If you are considering committing to a relationship, this would be a very good time, as the relationship is likely to be long-lasting and successful.

REFLECTION

An impossible chasm seems to be set between yourself and another. Yet this gulf can be bridged. Be honest about what you feel, and see if such honesty brings a change on the other side. Even if it does not, you will have acted appropriately.

The prince's court housed three thousand guests,
Nobody could say which was the greatest.
One of them complained of being ignored,
Claiming his worth was above all others.

TRADITIONAL INTERPRETATION

You should contemplate carefully the ramifications of any plan you attempt at the moment, as well as heeding the advice of others. If travelling, you are likely to experience many inconveniences and delays. Relationships will probably be happy and contented, and there is little chance of accident or illness within your family. You, however, should take care to keep healthy.

REFLECTION

No detail is too small, no concern too minor, to ignore at present. If you try to do things on too grandiose a scale, you may by accident ignore those of true worth while leaving yourself open to attack by the pompous and the ignorant. Take care in all you do. Focus on quality, not quantity. Listen, watch, be available, and you may be able to undertake great things without losing either yourself or others.

Reflections in rippling water,
Are constantly shifting, never the same.
In fate, though, everything is set,
And no advice can help the outcome.

五十四

TRADITIONAL INTERPRETATION

Like a reflection in water, your safety is not certain. You should take precautions against possible dangers, and not embark on any risky endeavors. In doing business, you will probably meet with many obstructions, and it is not a good time to put new plans into effect. Generally, things are likely to turn against you unless you keep tight control. On the positive side, you should recover from illness easily, and people missing from your life are likely to return soon.

REFLECTION

Chinese notions of fate and fortune set a clear line between that which is fixed and that which is changeable. Certain aspects of fate, like your date of birth or the kind of family you are born into, are fixed. The rest is up to you. However, if there is some aspect of yourself that makes you behave in a way you dislike, it is up to you to change. Otherwise you will 'fate' yourself to be like that for the rest of your life. Fate can keep you trapped. Your choice to change can set you free.

The Chief Minister was the wisest of all men.
Loved by good people; feared by the unjust.
He promoted honesty throughout the land
And advised the people to attend to their farms.

TRADITIONAL INTERPRETATION

Try to attend to your own home rather than putting all your energy into work, and do not crave for more money and status than you already have. It is a good idea to settle any outstanding disputes; otherwise they will likely be resolved against you. You are likely to remain in good health for a long time, and someone long absent from you may soon return.

REFLECTION

Good ministers and honest judges were highly honored in ancient China, and after death, they were often made judges in the afterlife. To be given good advice by such a person was to be given the wisdom of Heaven. And the usual advice, as in the Tao Te Ching, was to be content with what you have. Stop trying to find greener pastures. Live at ease with who and what you are.

56

The hidden dagger in water becomes a dragon,
Soaring far into the sky over thousands of miles.
A story like this can mean nothing but good.
You will rise higher as the result of an ordeal.

五十六

TRADITIONAL INTERPRETATION

While a significant test is approaching in your life, you will gain enormously if you succeed in it. This is a very opportune time to put any plans into action. Although you will encounter difficulties, remember that persistence is the best solution – splendid opportunities await you, and you can persevere despite your troubles. Events may take some time to turn to your advantage, but eventual success and a happy life are most likely.

REFLECTION

Whatever is troubling you now will (if handled well) become a source of great joy and success for you. The dagger symbolizes the danger or problems you currently face. The dragon symbolizes the ability to rise above your present circumstances and emerge triumphant.

Close your ears to rumour and scandal;
Your lot is a harvest of food and fine clothes.
Put all sorrow and woe out of your mind,
Place your trust in me and joy will be yours.

TRADITIONAL INTERPRETATION

This fortune is like a mother's lullaby to her baby. Just as a devoted mother cradles and protects her child, so you are protected by fate. Everything is well looked after at the moment, so you should have very few worries. It is wise to stay where you are and avoid travel, as your current situation is so well-favored by fortune. Also, it would probably be a good idea to make long-term investments.

REFLECTION

Think not of what others say, but remain true to the child within. Have faith. Trust those around you who have your best interests at heart. Ignore those who try to provoke you or who offer suspect advice. Listen to your conscience and your heart, and find the right way forward.

One state stood above the other six
And sought to conquer the whole of the land.
But one man united the six together,
And resisted the aggression of the seventh.

TRADITIONAL INTERPRETATION

This is a very promising fortune, but your fate ultimately lies with your own ability to make decisions and take the initiative. You should strive to be firm and assertive in order to overcome your problems. Although you may be suffering from illness now, it is not likely to have serious consequences. Now is a very good time to form close personal relationships.

REFLECTION

The brutal triumph of the Chin Emperor in 221 BC has left a deep scar on the Chinese psyche. The Chin kingdom defeated the other kingdoms and crushed all resistance. Thus this poem, which says what might have been, warns you to resist the growth of threatening forces by cooperating with others in the same situation. To allow division and disagreement to stand in the way of united opposition would be to leave yourself vulnerable to attack and takeover.

59

五十九

A simple maid was married to a noble lord,
Her perfect beauty proved the ruin of the king.
Another, though ugly, tried to match her smile.
But can the pheasant wear the phoenix's clothes?

TRADITIONAL INTERPRETATION

This is generally a precarious and tricky time for you, and it would be a very bad idea to make new plans. Any wealth you are enjoying at the moment is likely to be wasted, unless you invest it wisely. You should pay more attention to your health, or you may suffer considerable pain. The best way to find peace for yourself and avert these problems is to perform good deeds for others.

REFLECTION

The infamous courtesan who drains the powers of the decadent Emperor is a common story of the demise of various dynasties. This is a warning to avoid people who might divert you from what is right and proper. Be yourself, warts and all, as trying to be something that you are not is a true recipe for disaster.

六十

As a blazing fire consumes the fuel around it,
Spreading far and wide and sparing nothing,
So a fearful death awaits every one of us.
Neither rank nor riches can save us now.

TRADITIONAL INTERPRETATION

Any problems that occur are soon likely to become positive disasters unless you are very careful. Act quickly to stop problems getting out of your control, or they will become like the blazing fire described in the fortune. Minor health problems may develop into serious illness. Be cautious; and remember that what appears wise to you now may be foolish with hindsight. Listen closely to the advice of others.

REFLECTION

Life ends; this is a reality. In the end, we need to go into that dark night. You can try and resist, but eventually death awaits us all. As you draw near, look to what will be remembered of you when you are gone. Never mind power and wealth. Will you be missed for who you are? Will people mourn your passing because their lives will be the poorer for your absence?

61

六十一

The oracle is ambiguous; who can read it?
To some it means rebel and you will succeed.
But the honest general read it otherwise,
And found to his cost that this meaning was true.

TRADITIONAL INTERPRETATION

Your future teeters on a thin line between prosperity and disaster. Any decision you make now may well affect your life forever, but leaving things as they are will only make affairs worse. Do not act rashly; consider plans carefully before rushing into disaster. Calamity may well be prevented only at the very last moment.

REFLECTION

Not all divination can reassure. Sometimes you will be brought face to face with harsh, painful decisions; perhaps the very opposite of what you had hoped. Bite the bullet, and face the consequences. Do not dodge the difficult, but deal with it instead.

Holding a piece of fine jade is a rare treat.
It should be valued and loved as a worthy item.
Only great wealth can buy such beauty;
Great things deserve great honour, after all.

TRADITIONAL INTERPRETATION

While your current goal (whether it is recovering from sickness, making a long journey, or starting a business) will take a long time to succeed, patience will eventually lead to affluence. Profits, both financial and personal, may seem small at the moment, but they will eventually accumulate into great riches. Let reason and logic be your guide, and wait for the perfect moment to put a plan into effect.

REFLECTION

You have been privileged, but do not think it will last forever. Good fortune is like a piece of jade. The rare jade has passed through many hands of many centuries – those who thought they owned it are dust now, but the jade still exists. Treat fortune like that, and recognize that it passes on to others and is only with you for a moment.

63

六十三

Last time we sailed we lost our compass;
Today we set forth to search for it again.
Though the first compass was later found,
It is no use now and all hope is drowned.

TRADITIONAL INTERPRETATION

Misfortune is very close, and your current efforts to prevent it are useless. Forget your old methods, and try a completely new approach, or you may end up in considerable trouble. You are more likely to find success in business than in your personal life. Remember that compromise is often the best solution to a dispute.

REFLECTION

This poem is a warning. You are very close to making the wrong decision. Passion, power, and excitement have already caused you to lose your way once. Do not do it again. Use the compass of your conscience to guide you into making the correct decision – walking the true Tao. To do otherwise, will be unfortunate.

*T**wo good friends were in business together;*
The richer gave the poorer a larger share.
Such virtue did not go unrewarded, and very soon
Both became ministers under the great king.

六十四

TRADITIONAL INTERPRETATION

Working together with others is your best hope for advancement and profit. Form close friendships, and affairs will be settled quickly. Great chances are very close, and you will soon receive pleasing news. Investments will most likely prosper, and you will recover from most illnesses quickly.

REFLECTION

Quiet acts of kindness may seem insignificant, but in fact, they make you into the sort of person that kings and emperors would like as a friend. Nothing is too small to count. Cultivate kindness and compassion in your life. Discover how this will bring you a better fortune, because it will make you a better person.

CHAPTER 4

Taking Your Reading Further – The I-Ching Way

You now have your reading – perhaps two or three. Some light has been shed but you may want to go further. Obviously you can do this, but avoid trying to seek more insights, more revelations, if what you are really doing is running away from the reading! No matter how many oracles you consult, at the end of the day you have to make up your own mind. However, there are other steps you can take.

The sixty-four divination poems in Chapter 3 mirror the sixty-four hexagrams of the most powerful of oracles, the I-Ching *(see also page 13)*, and sixty-four divination sticks are used because of this strong association. It is not unusual for people seeking advice to consult simultaneously both a divination poem and the I-Ching. For the first time, we bring the two divination systems together in this pack, making cross-references between the two systems much easier.

You need not throw special divination tools – sticks or coins, for example – to consult the I-Ching readings. Simply take the number you achieved for your divination poem reading, then look up the corresponding hexagram reading for the I-Ching listed in this chapter.

In the example we gave in Chapter 3, we asked whether to break off one relationship and start up another. The stick that fell out was number 37, so we looked up poem 37, which read:

A great scholar knows the laws of Nature,
Seeing that as you sow, so shall you also reap.
There is no use praying to Heaven for your sins.
You will only find redemption in righteous living.

Hexagram 37 (Chia Jen) in the I-Ching (main oracle) reads: 'The family. It is good if a woman behaves properly.' Put the two readings together, and we begin to get some quite clear guidance on the centrality of proper relationships and the importance of doing the right thing.

Listed below are the key readings for each of the sixty-four hexagrams. As the divination sticks only give you a number, this is all you need to refer to the relevant hexagram, so what follows are the original shamanic oracles that form the heart of the I-Ching. We hope they will add to your depth of understanding of the reading and bring you closer to the decisions you need to make. Remember that these key readings reflect traditional I-Ching advice and may seem a little odd if taken at face value in modern-day terms. Interpret what they say in terms of your own current situation; do not take them literally. *(See Further Reading on page 112 for recommended books on the I-Ching.)* NOTE: The Hanyu Pinyin spelling for each hexagram is included in brackets.

THE SIXTY-FOUR I-CHING READINGS

乾

HEXAGRAM 1 – CH'IEN (Qian)
The origin. Continuing through. Harmonious. Correct.

坤

HEXAGRAM 2 – K'UN (Kun)
Great success. A wise man is virtuous and proper, like a strong and gentle mare. When he is faced with a task, he can only succeed if he takes things slowly and carefully, not trying to be first. A wise man must remember to draw strength from proper conduct, and by doing this, he will be fortunate.

HEXAGRAM 3 – CHUN (Tun)
Birth pangs. He will be successful if he behaves properly. Beware of starting a new venture without giving it enough thought. It will be useful to enlist the help of an experienced person.

HEXAGRAM 4 – MENG (Meng)
Rebellious youth. I do not look for the rebellious and ignorant child; it is he who looks for me. When he asks me for an oracle I will answer him. But when he asks me a second and third time, he becomes a nuisance. I refuse to answer his requests. It is helpful to be consistent and well-behaved.

HEXAGRAM 5 – HSU (Xu)
Patience. Confidence and sincerity will bring prosperity. Virtue will encourage good fortune. There is much to be gained by crossing the great river.

HEXAGRAM 6 – SUNG (Song)
Contention. He is confident in the face of opposition. Respectful behavior will bring good fortune. If he persists to the bitter end, there will be misfortune. It is very helpful to see the great man. It is not a good idea to cross the great river.

师 HEXAGRAM 7 – SHIH (Shi)
The army. Everything is correct. Nothing will go wrong if the leader is wise and experienced.

比 HEXAGRAM 8 – PI (Bi)
Unity. There will be good fortune. When he asks the oracle about his fortune, he is reassured. Those who are concerned will gather together at the right time. Those who arrive late will be unlucky.

小畜 HEXAGRAM 9 – HSIAO CH'U (Xiao Chu)
Holding back the less able. Progress and prosperity will develop. Clouds approach from our lands to the west, but they do not bring rain.

履 HEXAGRAM 10 – LI (Lü)
Walking carefully. Although the man treads on the tiger's tail, he is not bitten. There is success.

泰 HEXAGRAM 11 – T'AI (Tai)
Benevolence. The lesser has disappeared, and the greater is yet to come. There will be success and good fortune.

否 HEXAGRAM 12 – P'I (Pi)
Obstruction. Evil men block the path of progress. Events turn out badly for the wise man even when he acts correctly. The great are leaving, and the less important ones are arriving.

同人 HEXAGRAM 13 – T'UNG JEN (Tong Ren)
Companions. Friends will be found in the remote countryside. He will be successful. It is helpful to travel across the great river. The wise man will reap rewards if he behaves correctly.

大有 HEXAGRAM 14 – TA YU (Da You)
Many possessions. It bodes well for him to have numerous possessions and great success.

谦 HEXAGRAM 15 – CH'IEN (Qian)
Modesty. The wise man will eventually succeed in everything.

豫 HEXAGRAM 16 – YU (Yü)
Enthusiasm. The time is right to appoint princes and give orders for the army to approach.

随 HEXAGRAM 17 – SUI (Sui)
Agreement. Great success. It is helpful to behave with propriety. There will be no mistakes.

蛊 HEXAGRAM 18 – KU (Gu)
Decay. Crossing the great river will bring good fortune. Check everything carefully three days beforehand and three days afterwards.

临 HEXAGRAM 19 – LIN (Lin)

To draw near. This is a time of great success, which is helped by good behavior. The eighth month is an unlucky time.

观 HEXAGRAM 20 – KUAN (Guan)

Examine. He washes his hands in preparation but has not yet made the sacrifice. His dignified appearance inspires confidence in others.

噬嗑 HEXAGRAM 21 – SHIH HO (Shi Ke)

Biting through. Success. It is helpful to use the law.

贲 HEXAGRAM 22 – PI (Bi)

To adorn. Success. There is little to be gained in giving him permission to undertake anything.

剥 HEXAGRAM 23 – PO (Bo)

Peeling or splitting. Moving anywhere achieves nothing.

复 HEXAGRAM 24 – FU (Fu)

Return. Success. The man travelling to and fro will not be disrupted. His friends come to him, and there is nothing wrong with this. It is in his way to come and go. He returns on the seventh day. It is helpful to have a place to stay, wherever that may be.

无妄 HEXAGRAM 25 – WU WANG (Wu Wang)

Not false. Great success. It is good to remain firm. He will be distressed if he is wild instead of upright. It is useless for him to try to go in any direction.

大畜 HEXAGRAM 26 – TA CH'U (Da Chu)

Great powers of domestication. It is helpful to stand firm. He is lucky when he does not eat with his family. It is helpful to cross the great river.

颐 HEXAGRAM 27 – I (Yi)

Taking nourishment. By behaving properly, there will be good fortune. Look at what we seek to nourish. People naturally seek nourishment.

大过 HEXAGRAM 28 – TA KUO (Da Guo)

Great experience. The main support is weak. It is helpful to move in any direction. There will be success.

坎 HEXAGRAM 29 – K'AN (Kan)

The watery depths are twofold. Have faith. He keeps his heart faithful and prospers. Whatever he does is worthwhile.

离 HEXAGRAM 30 – LI (Li)

To part. It is useful to stand firm and behave well. This will bring success. Take care of the cows. There will be good fortune.

咸

HEXAGRAM 31 – HSIEN (Xian)
All-embracing. It is helpful to stand firm and behave properly. Marriage to a young woman will be fortunate.

恒

HEXAGRAM 32 – HENG (Heng)
Constant. There will be success. There is no mistake. It is helpful to stand firm and behave righteously. It is helpful to go forward in any direction.

遯

HEXAGRAM 33 – TUN (Dun)
To hide. There will be success. There is a small advantage to be gained from being firm and behaving properly.

大壮

HEXAGRAM 34 – TA CHUANG (Da Zhuang)
Great strength. It is helpful to act properly and firmly.

晋

HEXAGRAM 35 – CHIN (Jin)
To advance. The vigorous noble. He uses his charm like a display of fine horses. Three times within the space of one day he is received by an audience.

明夷

HEXAGRAM 36 – MING I (Ming Yi)
Brightness dimmed. It is wise to appreciate the dangers and behave properly.

家人

HEXAGRAM 37 – CHIA JEN (Jia Ren)
The family. It is good if a woman behaves properly.

睽

HEXAGRAM 38 – K'UEI (Kui)
Opposition. There will be good fortune in minor matters.

蹇

HEXAGRAM 39 – CHIEN (Jian)
There are advantages in the southwest. There are no advantages in the northeast. It is helpful to see the great man. Behave properly and there will be good fortune.

解

HEXAGRAM 40 – HSIEH (Jie)
Let loose. There are advantages in the southwest. If there is nothing else to be done, there is good fortune in his returning. If he has to go anywhere, it will be more fortunate to travel early.

损

HEXAGRAM 41 – SUN (Sun)
Injured. Have confidence. There will be supreme good fortune and no regrets. Proper behavior is possible. It is good to advance when fully prepared. Two baskets of offerings may be better than expensive offerings.

益

HEXAGRAM 42 – I (Yi)
Increase. It is helpful to go forward with plans in mind. It is good to cross the great river.

夬

HEXAGRAM 43 – KUAI (Guai)
New outcome. He must display it in the king's court. He must speak confidently with strict regard to honesty. There is danger. It is not a good idea to tell the city, nor is it useful to rush to arms. It is helpful to carry on with plans already in action.

姤

HEXAGRAM 44 – KOU (Gou)
To meet. The woman is strong and tough. Do not get married to a woman like this.

萃

HEXAGRAM 45 – TS'UI (Cui)
To collect. Success. The king approaches the temple. It is good to see the great man. There will be success. It is good to behave properly. The use of large offerings brings good fortune. To move forward in any direction will also bring good fortune.

升

HEXAGRAM 46 – SHENG (Sheng)
Rising up. There will be great success. He tries to see the great man. He does not worry. Moving to the south will bring good fortune.

困

HEXAGRAM 47 – K'UN (Kun)
To surround and wear out. There will be success. Keep going. The great man has good fortune. There will be no mistakes. He has a speech to make, but he is not believed.

井

HEXAGRAM 48 – CHING (Jing)
The well. The town may be moved but the well may not. It does not shrink or grow. People come and go to draw water from the well. If they cannot quite reach the water with a rope, or if the bucket breaks, there will be bad fortune.

革

HEXAGRAM 49 – KO (Ge)
Change. He is believed in his own right time. There will be great success. It is helpful to behave properly. Any cause for regret disappears.

鼎

HEXAGRAM 50 – TING (Ding)
Ting, the three-legged cooking pot. Great fortune and success.

震

HEXAGRAM 51 – CHEN (Zhen)
Shock. Success. The shock comes, but he looks out and is seen with cheerful words on his lips. Although the shock terrifies everyone for a hundred miles around, he does not drop the sacrificial spoon and cup.

艮

HEXAGRAM 52 – KEN (Gen)
Resting. Resting his back, he is not able to feel his own body. He goes in the courtyard. He does not see his own people. There will be no mistakes.

渐

HEXAGRAM 53 – CHIEN (Jian)

Gradual development. The woman is married. There will be good fortune. It is helpful to behave properly.

归妹

HEXAGRAM 54 – KUEI MEI (Gui Mei)

Marrying the younger sister. Initiating actions will bring bad fortune. There are no advantages here.

丰

HEXAGRAM 55 – FENG (Feng)

Prosperity. Success. There is nothing to worry about because the king achieves everything. He should be like the sun at midday.

旅

HEXAGRAM 56 – LU (Lü)

The traveller. Minor success. If the traveller behaves properly there will be good fortune.

巽

HEXAGRAM 57 – SUN (Xun)

Gentle and yielding. Minor success. It is helpful to advance. It is also helpful to see the great man.

兑

HEXAGRAM 58 – TUI (Dui)

Happiness. Success. It is advantageous to behave properly and firmly.

涣

HEXAGRAM 59 – HUAN (Huan)

Scattered. Success. The king travels to his temple. It is helpful to cross the great river. It is also good to behave properly.

节

HEXAGRAM 60 – CHIEH (Jie)

Limitations. Success. If the limitations are too strict, they should not be allowed to go on for too long.

中孚

HEXAGRAM 61 – CHUNG FU (Zhong Fu)

Inner confidence. Pigs and fish mean good fortune. It is helpful to cross the great river. It is helpful to behave properly.

小过

HEXAGRAM 62 – HSIAO KUO (Xiao Guo)

Minor problems. Success. It is useful to behave properly. This is appropriate for minor things but not for more important matters. The bird on the wing brings the message. It is good to come down but not to go up. There will be extremely good fortune.

既济

HEXAGRAM 63 – CHI CHI (Ji Ji)

Already done. Minor success. It is helpful to behave properly. There will be good fortune to begin with, but chaos at the end.

未济

HEXAGRAM 64 – WEI CHI (Wei Ji)

Not yet done. Success. A young fox crossing the stream gets his tail wet. There is no advantage in this.

CHAPTER 5

Hearing the Voices – Understanding Yourself

The divination poems draw upon ancient symbols, events, and images of China to convey the depth of their insights. To many Chinese, these images and events will be part of their common history, not unlike someone in the West saying, 'I don't know him from Adam,' or using the image of Noah's ark when talking about conservation. Similarly, the poems are part and parcel of the background and context within which the Chinese grow up.

VOICES UNKNOWN AND UNFAMILIAR

Increasingly, however, young Chinese people are unaware of this background. Communism and capitalism between them provide the strongest pulls for many of them and have removed much of traditional Chinese culture from their day-to-day experience. For a Western audience, a related problem arises: the poems' references and images are not familiar, so much of their power remains hidden or unknown.

We have tried to address this familiarity problem in the reflection part for each of the poems. In this chapter we take you a little deeper, providing a broader context within which to understand (and therefore draw much more from) the particular poem the sticks have given you.

The sixty-four poems are often very beautiful pieces of writing in themselves, sensitive, and full of the power of the muses. Many Chinese simply read the poems, selecting one to read a day. Rather than referring to them for divination or fortune-telling purposes, they see them as a source of inspiration, pausing to reflect and allowing themselves a little quiet time. We strongly recommend using the poems in this way.

The poems fall into three main types, each of which offers a distinctive way of looking at life, understanding yourself and the world around you.

THE COSMIC SETTING

The first poem type draws on the deep philosophical background of Taoism, of yin and yang, and of the cosmos as a setting and context for their wisdom. These poems tell you that they come from and draw you

back to this Ultimate Reality. Through symbols of difficulty, of struggle, contention and diversity, they say that the world never has been (and never will be) a happy and harmonious place, because life is made up of the dynamic of a struggle between contending forces.

Some people find such a model disturbing, but they should not. It is saying that if we search for peace and harmony, we will always be disappointed. This is what the Buddha taught. The search for happiness leads only to sadness when that happiness proves to be always transient. Chinese cosmology does not offer happiness or harmony but a dynamic relationship with struggle that produces a balance between forces, and this is what the cosmic aspects of the poems are saying. View yourself as a conflict-resolver rather than someone who ought to be happy and who gets upset if this is not the case. Confront what has to be faced, deal with it, then move on – this is what the cosmic view of China says.

The Raven and the Rabbit

Poem number 18, for example, is only really understandable when set within the cosmos of Chinese belief. The raven and the rabbit are both heavenly creatures: the raven is associated with the sun; the rabbit, with the moon. But there is more to it than this.

The raven is a slightly sinister figure. One of the oldest stories of China concerns the great archer, Yi. Long ago, around 2300 BC, a dreadful drought afflicted China because, instead of one sun in the sky, nine suns rose each day, and their combined heat was destroying the land, the trees, the plants, the animals and birds, and, of course, the people. The Emperor Yao heard of a great archer, Yi, who was summoned to court. Yao ordered him to shoot the eight extra suns from the sky, so Yi drew back his bow and let fly the most mighty shot of his life. The arrow flew into the heavens, and suddenly one of the suns exploded and vanished from sight. The arrow plummeted downwards, and on the end of it, stone dead, was a huge, black raven. Yi fired seven more arrows until only one sun was left. Each time, the arrow fell to the ground carrying a dead raven pierced through the heart. So the sun's raven is a awesome creature.

Unlike the rabbit. Many tales have tried to explain how it ended up on the moon. One Buddhist story tells how one day the Buddha visited a wood. All the animals and birds of the forest brought a gift: the lion brought his roar; the hummingbird, a beautiful feather; and so on. But the poor rabbit had nothing to bring, so he came to the Buddha and offered himself as food for him, whereupon the rabbit killed itself and lay dead at the foot of the Buddha. The Buddha was so moved by this that he brought the rabbit to life and put him on the moon for all to see, as a reminder of selfless love. Ending up on the moon, the rabbit symbolizes immortality, so is very much a Taoist figure as well. He has a much more benevolent aspect than the raven of the sun.

The Dragon and the Phoenix

Cosmic imagery is also found in poem 21. Here marriage is likened to the ultimate union of yin and yang, symbolized most frequently by the cosmic forces of dragon and phoenix. Their usual position is in a dramatic (almost antagonistic) mode, the two creatures leaping at each other. Here the poem envisages the dragon and the phoenix wrapped around each other, embracing their differences and becoming one – as the ideal partnership is supposed to do. It is important to note that the distinctiveness of each is preserved: they remain yin and yang, phoenix and dragon. What has changed is that they mold to each other rather than face each other – a beautiful model of a relationship.

True Freedom, or Fate?

Popular folklore and fables from the mythic world of China also form part of this cosmic view. An ancient image, found in many texts for the soul's longing for true freedom, is the story of the monkey who wants freedom, not the slavish duty of being a pet, even if he is held by the most beautiful golden chain imaginable. No matter how wonderful the servitude is, it is still servitude.

This rebellion against power, control, and being controlled is common to many Taoist texts. In the fourth century BC, Chuang Tzu used similar imagery about being a sacrificial ox. When asked if he wanted to become prime minister, he likened this to being the sacrificial ox – it is chosen, well fed and cared for, but ultimately it has to surrender its life when the Emperor wants to make a sacrifice. Chuang Tzu saw the luxury of the ox in terms of the mud and cold experienced by a free ox wandering the forest, and said he knew which he would rather be. Poem 36 echoes all this, as do a number of other poems reflecting upon true freedom.

The notion of fate and free will and our relationship with Heaven is spelled out in no uncertain terms in poem 37, as discussed on page 98, while poem 40 reflects on the belief in the Mandate of Heaven. The right to rule of dynasties and Emperors is seen as a gift from Heaven – only the worthy are capable of living up to this mandate. When unworthy Emperors come along – when wars, famine, corruption, and vice get out of hand because of the weakness or lasciviousness of an Emperor – the Mandate of Heaven has obviously been withdrawn. Once this is believed, the people have the right, under Heaven, to overthrow the Emperor and find a new one. The Mandate of Heaven can descend again, on this new Emperor, and peace, order, prosperity, and honesty

may return to the land. The challenge of poem 40 is this: do not just take authority lying down; many people prefer a quiet life and so allow injustice to flourish. The Chinese worldview says that it may be necessary to overthrow that which dominates you in order to have a good life. It echoes the monkey and the golden chain motif in poem 36 – the need to take risks in real living rather than to become domesticated (but really enslaved).

Poem 51 puts another gloss on all this. It shows that life can indeed be hard, but that Heaven has a season for everything and that you will be able to rest and relax as well as struggle. Poem 60 then reminds us of the reality of death. This we cannot escape: it is the ultimate threat to myths of happiness. But if we approach death as we are taught to approach life – as a challenge – then we shall be able to rise to it. No one can escape death, but we can ask ourselves what kind of a person we will be when we die.

INSIGHT FROM THE PAST – GUIDES TO THE FUTURE

Poems of the second type are historical. Chinese history has been recorded for longer, and without any break, than any other extant culture, and the moral lessons drawn from history have always formed the basis of being an educated Chinese. In the translations and reflections in this book, we have tried to avoid too much historical data – names, dates, and so on – and have focused instead on the message, the reason the stories have been chosen.

The key stories concern proper human relationships and how these need to be based on honesty and integrity. For example, poem 4 shows how gossip, innuendo, and malice can destroy the strongest of strong men. The Chinese take on the saying 'Sticks and stones may break my bones, but words can never harm me' is this: no, you can fight sticks and stones, but it is harder to fight rumor and bad talk. This is a highly realistic picture.

Fight the Power

Taoists despise power and position, and this is another common theme. Poem 7 refers to Lu, who had attained great power but did not let it distract him from his real quest – the search for immortality. Worldly material things are ultimately useless, especially when compared to spiritual things and life. Keep the material in balance; otherwise it can destroy you. This is reinforced by poem 23, which spells out in no uncertain terms how the material world is ultimately worthless.

This view is balanced by two other insights. Poem 10 points out that if you expect only the bad to suffer you are being foolish. Even one of Confucius's most important and devout disciples was afflicted by leprosy. Spiritual merit is no more a guarantee of happiness than material possessions. Illness, distress, unhappiness – all are part of being human. The secret is to rise above them, to put them in context and to deal with them. Poem 13 offers another, relevant, insight: there are times when you have to put aside the pursuit of the personal (even the personal quest for immortality) and take up the challenge of responsibility. The secret with Grandfather Kiang is that he knew how to let go as well as how to take up responsibility, but do you?

Loyalty and Virtue

Poem 16 refers to one of the most famous legends of ancient China: the loyalty and integrity of Shun the Filial. Shun's mother died when he was very young, and his stepmother hated him, even turning his own father against him. His own family tried to kill him on various occasions, but all attempts failed. Shun, however, never complained, and when his stepmother was ill he cared for her loyally. Dealing with strife and trouble is what life is about. Never return evil for evil because you become evil as well. Through Shun's selflessness, his family all came to realize the errors of their ways.

A similar kind of story about faithfulness to virtue and integrity is told in poem 32, one of the most popular stories of loyalty. Su Wu was an ambassador sent by the Emperor Wu (who reigned between 141 and 87 BC) to negotiate the release of a high official, Li Ling, who had been captured by the Huns, then living in Mongolia. When Su Wu arrived, he discovered that Li Ling had gone over to the enemy and been rewarded with untold wealth. Su Wu was offered the same but he refused. The Huns punished him initially by casting him into a deep pit, and every day they asked him to betray his master. Every day he refused. After a few years they sent him to be a shepherd. Every year they brought him in rags to the palace and asked him if he would betray his emperor, and every year he refused. Eventually, nineteen years later, due to the military power of the Chinese, Su Wu was released and came home to great rejoicing, and the praise and thanks of the Emperor. Li Ling died a hunted man in the wastes of Mongolia.

To be that faithful is unusual today, as it was nearly two millennia ago. These types of stories ask us to think long and hard about putting ourselves first – not a popular message in the 'me' world of today, but perhaps one of the most important to come out of the poems.

Get Your Priorities Right

The quest for what is really important is a constant theme. Poem 31 puts it beautifully, talking of two scholars competing for the highest prize at the Imperial exams. This prize would bring vast financial

reward and power – which is why villages with a promising child in their midst would pool their resources to build him a special scholar's tower and provide him with the best tutors they could find. If and when he was successful in the exams, he would then be expected to share his financial success with the villagers.

But this poem makes a very different point. One of the scholars fails and thus has to return home to face the disappointment of his people. But he falls ill. When eventually he does get home, everyone is so relieved that he is still alive that they forget their disappointment. This poem says to keep things in perspective.

Be True to Your Beliefs

Finally, the poems point out one other great truth. Sometimes people have to work with others who either do not come up to their own standards or who simply do not understand why you do the things you do. Two of the divination poems capture this notion.

Poem 47 tells of the Emperor's envoy, who achieves amazing success in the name of the Emperor, but the Emperor knows he is incapable of living up to the envoy's expectations. Sometimes it is those above us who fail us. But this does not mean that we should cease to strive for the very best. The other example is poem 50. Here, a great hero (Kuan Ti) escapes and is ferried to freedom by one of his friends – a boatman. Kuan Ti offers his sword to the ferryman, but he declines to take it. The boatman does what he does because he shares the beliefs and values of the great hero, not because he wants reward.

Being misunderstood is common. Do not let this betray why you do what you do.

NATURE AS THE MIRROR OF YOUR SOUL

The third type of poem is that based on Nature. Throughout the divination poems there are gems of observation and reflection on Nature as a mirror of the Tao.

Poem 2 is a fine example. Here the coming of spring is celebrated as a wonder in its own right, but also as a metaphor for immortality and new birth. The link between the trees budding and the peach tree of immortality producing fruit (which only happens once every thousand years) is used to remind us that all the lost find their way home. In other words, you may be in the midst of bleakness and sadness now (the winter of your soul), but things do change – spring comes again.

In classic yin/yang style, this is immediately followed by poem 3. Here the struggles of a mother sparrow to protect her young are compared to the struggles of the traveller – you and I. What we build to defend and protect ourselves (physically as well as metaphorically) is subject to decay as well as change. In the end we are left exposed and vulnerable before Heaven.

Poem 8 takes opposite forces in Nature – here, birds and plants that do not mix – and uses them as an image of unnatural groupings. Do not bring things together that Nature has seen fit to keep separate.

Sometimes the poems just love to picture us in Nature, and poem 11 is a delightful example. Here there is no particular symbolism; simply a sense of wonder in Nature and in the ease of human living. Similar to this, but with a little twist at the end, is poem 14, which celebrates being in Nature but ends with a sting: Nature itself is not always paradise!

Nature is also used to evoke moods, as in poem 26. Shadows, moon and the 'crane's mournful cry' are used to intimate the coming of night and the need for the traveller to hurry home. Eating as a part of the joys of Nature is also celebrated (as in poem 29), while the simpler things of life form the heart of poem 38, where the poet as worker is beautifully juxtaposed with the quest for peace, quiet, and reflection. The attempt to make Nature into something it is not is one of our favorite images: poem 39 describes polishing a stone and trying to turn it into a mirror! In an age where we think technology or even just sheer willpower can transform one thing into something else, this is a vital reminder of the inherent integrity of things.

BRINGING YOURSELF TO THE POEM

Whole books have been written on the use of imagery in Chinese poems and divination. In this chapter we have tried to give you a sense of the depths lying beneath the deceptively simple poems.

The poems can speak in other ways, too. You bring to them your own experiences, your own culture and beliefs. You have visions and dreams, histories and images, and these speak to you, perhaps even without you knowing this. Bring all these ideas to the divination readings, and you will find greater insights there.

Maybe you will be moved to write your own poetry. This is an age-old way of responding to divination poems. Allow the thoughts and ideas, hopes, and aspirations that have brought you to seek the help of the oracle to express themselves in poetic form. Poems can often express what we otherwise find impossible to say.

In bringing yourself to the poem as well as allowing the poem to bring its wealth of imagery, insight and knowledge, you are acting in a truly yin/yang fashion. From this dynamic, new ways of understanding can come about. Yes, even a new you!

FURTHER READING

PLEASE NOTE: All books are listed with their first publication date, and were in print at the time of going to press.

The Book of Chuang Tzu, translated by Martin Palmer with Elizabeth Breuilly. London: Penguin Arkana, 1996.

A Dictionary of Chinese Symbols, Wolfram Eberhard. London: Routledge & Kegan Paul, 1983.

The Elements of Taoism, Martin Palmer. Shaftesbury: Element Books, 1991.

Essential Chinese Mythology, Martin Palmer and Zhao Xiaomin. London: Thorsons, 1997.

The Feng Shui Kit, Man-Ho Kwok. London: Piatkus Books/Boston: Charles E. Tuttle Co. Inc./Singapore: Asiapac Books. 1995.

Hsun Tzu, translated by Burton Watson. New York: Columbia University Press, 1963.

I Ching, translated by Martin Palmer, Jay Ramsay and Zhao Xiaomin. London: Thorsons, 1995.

Kuan Yin, Martin Palmer, Jay Ramsay and Man-Ho Kwok. London: Thorsons, 1995.

Ling Ch'i Ching, translated by Ralph D. Sawyer and Mei-chun Lee Sawyer. Boston: Shambala, 1995.

The Lotus of the Wonderful Law, translated by W. E. Soothill. Oxford: Clarendon Press, 1930.

Monkey, translated by Arthur Waley. London: Penguin Classics, 1942.

Romance of the Three Kingdoms, translated by C. H. Brewitt-Taylor. Boston: Charles E. Tuttle Co. Inc., 1959.

The Shambala Guide to Taoism, Eva Wong. Boston: Shambala, 1997.

Sources of Chinese Tradition, Volumes I & II, Wm. Theodore de Bary, Wing-Tsit Chan and Burton Watson. New York: Columbia University Press, 1960.

Spirit Token of the Ling Qi Jing, Ivan Kashiwa. New York: Weatherhill, 1997.

Tao Te Ching, translated by Man-Ho Kwok, Martin Palmer and Jay Ramsay. Shaftesbury: Element Books, 1993.

The Rise of a Refugee God – Hong Kong's Wong Tai Sin, Graeme Lang and Lars Ragvald. Hong Kong: Oxford University Press, 1993.

Yin and Yang, Martin Palmer. London: Piatkus Books, 1997.

ACKNOWLEDGMENTS

AUTHORS' ACKNOWLEDGMENTS

We would like to thank our families, and in Xiaomin's case to celebrate the arrival of his daughter during the writing of this book. We also owe a great debt to our colleagues at ICOREC, especially Joanne Robinson, Gena Darwant and James Palmer, without whose help this could never have been finished on time. Finally, a thank you to the many fortune tellers and Taoists in China who have shed so much light on this subject for us during our travels together across China. Too many to name, they know how much we have enjoyed their company.

EDDISON•SADD EDITIONS

Editorial Director.......................... Ian Jackson
Senior Editor............................. Tessa Monina
Project Editor......................... Nikky Twyman
Proofreader............................. Michele Turney
Art Director......................... Elaine Partingto
Mac Designer.......................... Brazzle Atkin
Illustrator.............................. Julie Carpente
Production................................. Cara Herro

The illustrations on pages 11 and 34–97 are reproduced by kind permission of CIRCA Photo Library at ICOREC.